Teacher

Potty M...

Another anecdotal memoir from the world of education

By Maxine Blake

Truth.

This is the truth. Well, as I see it anyway.

Teacher Bloopers and Potty Mouth Stories

First published by MaxineBlake.com 2023

A catalogue record of this book is available from the British Library First edition.

Paperback ISBN: 978-1-8383040-3-4

Cover art by David Fenton
Editing by Rebecca Wojturska
Illustration by Jo Titman
Typesetting by David Fenton

For Jody

TABLE OF CONTENTS

PREFACE

During his competitive volleyball years many moons ago, my brother would often retort,

'I've only got one set in me.'

I felt the same way about my book. I was adamant that it was a 'one-off. I retired from teaching in 2020, but, as with the rest of the world, the emergence of COVID severely curtailed my options. My choices were confined to traveling as far as my feet could carry me from my front door. My son's constant mantra of:

'The world needs to read your stories,'

Finally led to the publication of my first book in 2020.

What's important to know about me, is that I'm not the type to throw caution to the wind. I'm a typical non-risk taker with a glass-half-full outlook. How I ever managed to press the publish button, I will never know. I braced myself for the inevitable not-so-positive feedback and mentally hunkered down to defend myself. But you have to start somewhere, the only way is up, right? To my surprise, messages from readers arrived, expressing their joy on reviving some of their forgotten memories, whilst offering their own funny stories. Others recalled their own experiences, or their relatives' teaching days and admired my courage in sharing the stories of my most humiliating moments. People in my neighbourhood often stopped me, asking, 'Are you the 'Don't Poo' author?' My reluctance to answer was often ignored, as they continued to share tales from their years in education. The seeds for Book 2 were planted.

The publication of 'Don't Poo in the Pudding Bowl' brought with it additional unexpected surprises. I reconnected with long-lost colleagues from up to forty years ago; spent many evenings reminiscing about the good old days and how we managed to survive them. They also reminded me of forgotten stories. So I began to record them for possible future use. My life has been enriched by reconnections with people from far and wide, reminding me of how education can be life-changing, and how we, as educators, are privileged to be in such an influential position.

In my first book, I frequently mentioned my boys. This time, the girls have taken centre stage. The pivotal moment occurred when I reconnected with some of my former pupils from 1983, they have now become a vibrant group of women, each carving their own unique paths in life. They, in turn, provided their versions of some of my accounts. There are three sides to every story...' As the old saying goes. I uncharacteristically took a risk and have been repaid in abundance.

It's a struggle, but I'm still learning.

Part 1: Perspectives

NAVEL GAZING

A brief introduction to John

He was a polite softly spoken member of staff. There was the perpetual sense that he was merely passing through the college. To coin a phrase, he was never going to get his feet firmly ensconced under the table. He dressed neatly, and his attire rarely attracted unwanted attention, except on a few occasions. When he exercised in the gym, somehow his sense of dress would become, as I would like to express, a little retro. Maybe from the 70's short-shorts era. His exercise methods were interesting too, but he never asked for advice, so none was ever given.

His personal attire attracted a certain level of interest that was not always complementary.

On one such day, his pink and blue striped shirt stretched tightly about his torso, providing a hallucinatory effect on my brain. It was clear to see that a fight had developed along his front. The angle of view was unfortunate, as my eyes immediately latched onto the hairs poking through at the top of his shirt, they then involuntarily wandered down its seam, mesmerised as each of the buttons were skew-whiff and had given up their fight to keep the stripes in alignment. The tension came to a stand-off at his stomach. Each button threatened to pop at the slightest movement of his midsection. The hairs fought to gain prominent positions through the buttonholes. They peered through in ever-increasing clusters and amassed at his navel. A thought crossed my mind,

'If I poked my finger in...

Bile immediately rose from my stomach, and I tasted the acidity in my throat. I fought to shift the image from my brain.

... how much of my finger would I lose?' (Urgh! my hands twitched in protest)

Let me take you back a few steps.

I was completing a teaching observation with Hayley, my colleague in an IT suite; not an ideal situation, but the college classrooms were at full capacity that day. The lesson to be taught was entitled: 'Preparing for an Interview.' Prior to entering the room, we had discussed our approach, the areas of focus and the incorporation of any concerns from his previous observation. Having agreed on these, we knocked and waited. John, the teacher, opened the door, we entered the room, I took the left side, and Hayley the right, ensuring that our views spanned the whole of the class. A few of the students were already seated and were scattered around idly conversing with each other. Our presence immediately dulled their conversations. We sat and stared above the computer screens whilst the late comers slipped apologetically into the room. John narrowed his eyes and shot metaphorical daggers towards them. He bared his teeth, was that a grimace or a smile? He quickly ushered them to their seats.

Despite our strategic positioning, our view of some of the students were somewhat limited; we could only see the tops of their heads, heaven knows what they were really doing at their screens. Unfortunately, my view of John was not as restricted. My head swivelled towards my colleague, we exchanged glances, she reacted with a wide-eyed stare. John walked down one of the aisles looking from side to side as he quickly began his introduction. Hayley and I followed his path but were instantly transfixed on one point.

His navel.

I was staring again. Questions raced through my mind:

'Why is navel fluff always blue? Is it? Well, that's what I've been told. Is this true of all races? Mine's button-shaped so it collects nothing. It had never occurred to me to ask anyone.'

My mind digressed. I forced my thoughts back to the lesson at hand. Focussing on the task had become impossible as my mind was racing through a million scenarios, none of them educational.

The lesson was uneventful. Well, our lack of ability to focus past John's state of dress meant that much of its content could not be recalled. We nodded at each other to signal that the observation was over, and we took our leave. We smiled and thanked the teacher and students for having us, as if they had any choice in the matter. I closed the door behind me.

We exhaled and identified the nearest empty room to allow ourselves the privacy needed for such a delicate matter. What on earth was that? We had found very little information relating the lessons' content with the students' levels of learning. As we continued to compare our observations, we smiled as we noted the common factors on each of our files: the endless doodles of hair and wavy stripes had occupied the margins.

Can you downgrade for inappropriate clothing?

WELLBEING DAY, BUT FOR WHOM?

A brief introduction to Louise

She was a tall, confident member of staff. She was tech savvy and quite creative when it came to the dreaded timetabling tasks. She knew what she wanted and would not be held back in her quest for achievement. Her language could be a little ornate at times, much to the chagrin of others, and she took no prisoners. She was always on the go, had charts, folders and books for every eventuality. Her mind was always working overtime. Her facial expressions told you all that you needed to know.

The college had been implementing a concept called 'Wellbeing Day' for some time now, the staff welcomed this as it was a time to let our hair down and relax at the end of the year. The idea behind it was that after a hard year of work, we deserved a little rest and recuperation by spending quality time with our colleagues for the whole day or however much we desired.

Kevin, one of our colleagues, didn't understand this concept, he firmly stated that he was paid to work so that's what he was going to do. Bonding with staff outside of the work environment was not his forte. He found the idea hellish and would rather be left alone in his gym office to complete his work. He managed to accomplish this for many years. He argued, if we wanted to improve staff wellbeing, then we should have the right to choose the manner in which it was to be taken; this was his choice after all.

The main requirement from the principal was that we took time out to enjoy each other's company wherever and however we saw fit. In addition to this, we had the option to share our jollies by way of producing photographic evidence for the college website and social media platforms. Staff were free to offer their areas of expertise and lead the groups in numerous activities, so the ideas were varied and extensive. The options ranged from camping trips, walking, cricket, lunch, the spa, shopping and the pub. If you offered to lead the activity and the staff signed up, then it was highly likely to go ahead.

John held a regular guest spot on a weekend radio show as a Colour Analyst and decided that he would offer his expertise to any colleagues who wished to take him up on his offer. In an effort to persuade staff to join him for retail therapy at our local out-of-town shopping centre, he promised to provide hands-on advice by matching appropriate fashion, colours and styles to his peers natural colouring in order to boost their self-confidence and allow for a positive transformation. Through his radio interviews, listeners would contact him and ask for advice on their wardrobes. They would happily hear his solutions when he advised them of the perfect colours to complement their skin tones. A perfect activity for some, but for me this would have been a recipe for disaster. I take any criticism of my attire as a direct attack on myself, so as you may gather, this was not an option that I would be pursuing at any given time.

Two colleagues, who were also very close friends, decided that this was the perfect day for them. What could be better than to stroll around shops with your personal dresser? The day arrived and John, the Colour Analyst, presented himself nice and early. He signed the college's attendance sheet and retrieved his list ready to meet his new clients. His outfit consisted of a pair of Nike toe-trainers; sand-coloured skinny trousers held in place with a Gucci belt. A multi-coloured t-shirt that appeared to be just a little on the tight side, and a neat man-bag perched delicately across his shoulders. This ensemble was topped off with a nifty black flat cap, set at a jaunty angle. He was all set to provide his first instructions of the day. *'Interesting choice of clothing.'* I thought.

With his patrons now gathered, he explained the first task of the day. They were to complete a questionnaire about their dress habits. The forms were completed and returned to him, after which, having read through them, he delivered a quick private critique to each person on what they were currently wearing, including types of clothing and their colour choices. The critique was provided to focus on his suggested colour schemes and shapes of clothing they would be advised to buy from that day forward. Having purchased items based on his feedback, he would then review their improved choices.

Louise had carefully chosen her wardrobe that morning and arrived in a long black belted dress. She knew that this suited her as she had often been told how it made her look wiser with a sense of authority. She had always accepted this comment gracefully. Using a combination of her questionnaire with a review of her skin, hair and eyes; John then produced a colour chart. As a result of his analysis, she should be wearing cool colours, such as green, purple or blue. She internalised his advice and after much thought, responded by stating that coral was a strong favourite of hers. She was fully aware that this was not in the 'cool colours' bracket. His tone and response was probably not what she had expected to hear.

"Definitely not."

This probably flew out of his mouth a little quicker than he expected.

Would he have replied in a similar manner to the queries whilst on-air? Somehow, I doubted it.

Louise was not usually the type of person to take this advice lightly. Surprisingly, she found herself unable to respond to his rebuttal. Along with her friend, she found her only reaction was to march towards her car, internalising her rage. She saved her profanities until she had exited the building. Their Wellbeing Day had just taken a very sharp U-turn. They arrived at the shopping centre with a heightened sense of focus. She knew what she had to do.

The following day was the last day of term and with no students present, it took on the atmosphere of dress-down Fridays. Not so for Louise, she announced her arrival in the college building dressed head to toe in coral. She stopped to pass pleasantries with staff in the presence of John, she politely acknowledged his presence but ignored any requests to review the previous day's activities. Well, not within his earshot anyway.

Suffice it to say, no further advice was ever sought from John.

A THORN IN MY SIDE

I walked into my classroom, as usual the students meandered in after me. They rarely wanted to be indoors. They lived for football, whether it was playing, watching, criticising, or simply admiring it, they could turn any conversation into a football-focused one before I could inhale. Their constant attempts to engage me in conversations of the football kind often left them frustrated and bemused. My response would often be along the lines of,

"Oh, is there an important match this weekend?"

They would look at me incredulously and wonder how any living person could have no interest in 'the beautiful game.' I knew how to wind them up and took pleasure in this.

I held little interest in the intricacies of football, so their attempts at converting me were always futile. They knew this but would continue with their bids nonetheless.

They would always lose the battle and eventually relent, sit down and happily engage with each other instead. This ritual continued throughout the year. The usual preambles of attendance checking, and general chit-chat would then take place.

Then came that interruption.

"Hey, Maxine, I saw you in McDonald's the other day."

Everything stopped.

A deathly silence filled the room. All eyes were transfixed on me, then swivelled around towards Duncan.

They waited for the usual battle to begin.

I heard mutterings of,

"That's it, he's gone too far now."

I raised my eyebrows.

Additional remarks filtered through,

"Naw, man, you know she ain't into all a dat."

"Maybe she's turned."

"Never, you know how she bangs on about good food. She ain't 'bout dat."

"So, you saw me inside a McDonalds, did you? Which one was it?"

"The one on Granville Road, innit?"

He paused.

The noise of chairs scraping on the floor filled the air as the class turned around and vied for the best viewing spot. This was going to be good.

"Well," he paused. "When I say in McDonalds…"

His speech slowed down, and he began to whisper, or was it a whimper?

"I saw you walking past it… You were close though."

He looked around and grinned at the class.

The tension dissipated and with it an audible sigh of relief flooded the room.

"Idiot," a student announced.

'Nuff said,' I thought.

HAS IT GONE A LITTLE TOO FAR?

"Maxine?"

"Yes?

"You know lots about the body, don't you?"

"Well, I suppose I do."

I was flattered by the compliment. I waited for the caveat.

The young male student slowly peeled his t-shirt up. I looked on, frozen in the moment,

"I have this lump on my chest, can you have a look please?"

Words failed me. My eyes dipped to the protruding lump before setting themselves in constant motion between his face and the disturbing overhang from his left pectoralis just below his nipple.

He was testing me. As I studied the form, he hoisted his shirt further up and placed a section in his mouth, to provide an effective comparison of both sides I presumed. He knew that I was transfixed; he carefully placed both hands on his hips and began to flex and contract his pectorals, alternating them up and down as though he was posing in a bodybuilding competition. His new appendage appeared to wobble in the upward phase, then cling on for dear life as his left pec relaxed.

I remained in position. The lump reminded me of ganglions that often appeared on wrists. I recalled that a home remedy was to bash it with a book, preferably a Bible. I've no idea why.

I could not summon up a Bible, but a hefty physiology book could do the trick. It was so tempting.

His pecs stopped.

He jutted his neck out and gave me a little nod in anticipation. No further utterance escaped his mouth. I took the bait.

"Did that arise as a result of a sporting activity?"

"Well, no, but..."

"Aah."

I swiftly interrupted him.

"I only assess sporting injuries. That..."

I circled the perimeter of the alien on his chest and eyeballed it. I'm sure that it was moving of its own volition.

"...is way out of my jurisdiction. I strongly suggest that you phone your GP today. Now please put it away."

I swiftly aborted the conversation as I was losing the battle with the nausea moving through my stomach and making its way up my gastrointestinal tract.

How would he react if I projectile vomited over his bare chest, never mind onto his newly attached friend?

***

A brief introduction to Aftab

He was very well-mannered and was always the first student to arrive at the classroom door. Here, he would ceremoniously open the door for staff and offer to carry their bags to their desks. He would often engage in conversation about his homeland in Eastern Europe whilst the staff prepped for their lessons. He never seemed to put a foot wrong.

He always presented himself impeccably, both in his manner and dress. He appeared to be the ideal student.

In the evenings when he was due to attend his cadet's meetings, he would make a point of wearing his uniform to college for his lectures. He knew that it was against cadet rules. Equally, he knew that he would be drawing just the right kind of attention from the staff as well as the young female students. He had enrolled on our Public Services course, and we presumed that towards the end of his studies, he would apply for a post in a similar field. He would often retort that he was the ideal army or navy candidate. He mentioned this when the principal made one of his impromptu classroom visits. On this day, as he sat behind his desk, his highly polished shoes and bright white socks attracted our attention. I glanced down and noticed that he was wearing an electronic tag. This is used to monitor curfews and is handed out as a condition of a police or court order. The look on my face directed the principal's eyes downwards. He had noticed it too.

I wondered then whether his insistence on the army or navy as a career option was more a case of Hobson's choice, as opposed to an actual career plan. I made a mental note to find out just how he fell from grace. I knew just the person to ask. My wonderful colleague Kevin: had always thought that there must be a chink in Aftab's armour and had been quite direct when he had expressed his suspicions. Having made him aware of my findings, he nodded, tilted his head and gave me that 'told you so,' look. No further words passed my lips.

"Leave it with me, Maxine."

Off he went in search of the evidence. I resumed my normal duties and impatiently waited for his return. Fortunately, the wait was minimal. He went straight to the source: the student files. When his research ground to a halt he must have grunted, as Sheila, who worked in admin, asked if she could help. He expressed his concerns. Much to his surprise, she uttered that she just happened to be in the vicinity when he arrived for his college interview with his social worker in tow and as it turned out, she somehow overheard him query whether he ought to declare his burglary conviction.

With that, Kevin gave Sheila a satisfied grin and walked away.

***

A brief introduction to Joe

He was a very tall, quiet, polite and unassuming member of staff. He knew everyone and studied people to the point of being able to mimic them with alarming accuracy. Despite his immense height, large family and numerous pets; his car purchases were perpetually on the small side. He was known over the years for being able to stuff himself into the smallest of vehicles and once he had arrived at his destination, he was able to unravel himself effortlessly from it, much to the admiration of his peers. He quietly beavered away at work; he didn't need to make loud noises to gain the attention of the students as his approach could be seen from afar.

Joe walked into reception as he needed to use the guillotine quickly before his next lesson. Dangling from its corner was a transparent folder containing some paperwork.

"What's this?"

"It's the new health and safety policy."

"For the guillotine? Has the world gone crazy?"

He proceeded to remove the paperwork from its poly pocket. He began to read it; his face contorted as his eyes sped their way down the page.

"I give up. You need a degree to read the actual policy on how to operate it. It's ridiculous."

With that, he unceremoniously stuffed the paperwork back in its pocket.

Our trusted colleague Sheila in admin, without whom the college would fall apart, could offer no further comment.

***

Trevor, the Health and Safety Officer who implemented *'The Guillotine Safety Manual Policy,'* thought it prudent to complete a spot check on students in their placement settings, just to ensure they were safe and complying with the college's health and safety procedures.

He arranged to visit one of the nearby primary schools and did not like what he saw at all. On his return from the placement, he immediately reported his findings to Louise, the Curriculum Lead for Health and Care. He appeared very agitated, and with little introduction, he advised that a student be withdrawn forthwith from the placement.

She expressed her deep concern and probed further to ascertain the exact nature of the problem. Noting that the look of consternation remained, she indicated that he should take a seat and make himself comfortable. Trevor complied. He looked toward her and proceeded to state his findings.

"As the college's 'ealth and Safety Officer, I must ensure that all the students' welfare, 'ealth and safety are effectively managed. In effect, where placements are compulsory, they also fall under the auspices of our 'ealth and safety policies."

She nodded her head whilst reminding herself that he was always fastidious in his explanations.

"You may 'ave noticed that I've recently created the new guillotine use policy."

Her eyebrows raised in anticipation.

Her facial gymnastics were rarely misinterpreted by her colleagues.

"Well, I wer' talking through t' policies with their designated 'ealth and Safety Officer and wer 'appy that I could sign off on all documents. I asked if I could check up on one of our students; as I were there it med sense."

He paused.

"Again, they wer 'appy for me to do that."

Louise leaned back, exhaled, and waited for the punchline.

"Our student marched over t' guillotine and started to use it," he paused again, "without supervision. I couldn't believe me eyes." His eyes widened. "I thought about saying sommat to er, then noticed one of the small kids ger up and shouted towards the teacher to ask if she needed to cut her paper. The teacher motioned her towards t' guillotine with a flick of 'er wrist, just reminding 'er to be careful. She didn't even look up! It looked as though this were a regular occurrence!"

She watched as his face contorted and at this point had now managed to match his blood-red clipboard. She was concerned for his physical health; he was almost blowing a gasket.

She adjusted her seat.

"I'm sure that you can see t' severite' of situation. I'll leave it in your capable 'ands."

He then stood up, noted her acknowledgement, and left the room.

Louise exhaled, scratched her head, and chuntered.

"For crying out loud, we 'ave guillotines all o'er the place. He's never been in any of the early years or art rooms. He's 'never taught anythin'. We'd never get any teaching done if we applied his rules."

Louise ignored his request.

FLYING BY THE SEAT OF YOUR PANTS

The post-it notes, complete with a range of questions from simple to complex, were stuck onto the windows outside my classroom door. At this point in the year, the students understood that the earlier they arrived at the door, the greater their choice of tasks would be. It's first come, first served. They filed in, some with triumphant smiles, waving their post-its in the air, the others already looking downtrodden, sunk into their allocated chairs to begin their tasks.

It was the day that I dreaded... Well, most teachers do. Not the Ofsted one, that's something way off the Richter scale altogether. Observation Day. This occurs frequently over the academic year, and it should be like water off a duck's back, but the apprehension and anxiety appears to increase when the observer is a fellow manager and colleague.

Upon being provided with my observation allocation window, I thought about the content of my lesson long and hard. Should I do something left of field and complete a mimed lesson where the students alone are vocal? Should I produce a singing lesson? I've often threatened the students with this idea, not too dissimilar to Buffy the Vampire Slayer's musical episode? Or should I just play it safe?

I'm not one for playing it safe. The grades were from 1 (Outstanding) to 4,(Inadequate). On good days I think I average at Grade 2. Like many teachers, on some days, I'd kick it out of the park and would classify myself at the highest level. The other days when it's not so great, well I'd rather not talk about them. For those in education when receiving feedback, we're told the grading is never about our performance as a teacher but about the student's progression. The comments received are often a blur from this point onwards. All that is usually heard is: 'Blah, blah, blah,' as we await our grades. The stock phrase is, 'It's about the development and distance travelled by the learner.' We always take it personally though. Don't we?

Back to the lesson, I had over-prepared as you do for such occasions and was ready, or as ready as I would ever be. Everything was set out in my room. I waited patiently. The students filed in, post-its in hand, and sat down, facing forwards. I greeted them and plied them with a few appropriate questions whilst they settled down to work on their tasks. They were just a little too mellow on the enthusiasm front and needed the occasional burst of fire under them to liven them up. My observer walked in, file in hand and I gave her the nod. The students looked at her, then at me and uncomfortably shifted in their seats. I reassured them by stating the usual:

"Don't worry, she's watching me, not you."

I needed to get into the full swing of the lesson. The register was taken, they were all here, and on time for once.

'That's always a good start.'

They appeared to be fully engaged discussing the answers to their post-it questions. I began to open the PowerPoint on my computer for the main section of the lesson. The focus was on nutrition. A few videos had already been uploaded. I clicked the remote control to turn on the projector, and it began to make its usual whirring noises as it warmed up, a little like flies being caught in the lampshade. We were used to that, but not for what happened next. The buzzing increased in sound and pace, then boom, a flash of lightning lit up the class quickly followed by what looked like silver confetti exploding from the ceiling, covering the students in front of me. Screams penetrated through the air, from me, the students, the observer, maybe everyone, I'm still unsure. The students looked at me, I looked at them, they knew that I occasionally surprised them with weird and wonderful activities for my starter sessions, but they quickly realised that this wasn't one of them. I looked up and noted that the projector was hanging limply from the ceiling. It was silent. Having scanned the room to make sure that the students were all fine. I thought,

'What the hell am I going to do now?

Plan B

What Plan B?

Oh my God, there's no Plan B.'

My colleague looked at me whilst I subconsciously wrestled with my nerves. She twitched in her chair.

"Just give me a minute."

I turned my back to the class, opened my mouth wide and mouthed a silent scream. I'm back in control... well, I willed myself to be, so I started to write on the whiteboard. I was buying myself some time. I began to write frantically, thinking of how to seamlessly incorporate an exploding projector into my lesson.

'How am I going to do this? What are the lesson aims again?'

I noted that the PowerPoint was still visible on the computer screen, so I took a sneaky peak. I needed to flip this lesson on its head quickly. I turned and noted that they had all downed tools to happily admire the new decorations that had infiltrated the room. It was in their hair, down their backs, on the desks, and all over the floor. Students were wriggling and sneezing as some had unfortunately snorted some of the content up their noses.

"Nice one Maxine, and it's not even Christmas."

"It's always phones away, no sweets, empty mouths, pen and paper out. Today it's like we've won the lottery."

I could not have disagreed with them there.

Inspiration can sometimes appear in the guise of defeat; and I still needed more thinking time.

"Ok, how did that make you feel?"

"What?

"How did that make you feel? "The semblance of an idea was taking shape. I seized the moment and ran with it.

Links to adrenalin and neurotransmitters circulated through my brain and emerged through my mouth immediately backed up with questions on the board. I clutched at the opportunity to relate the body's responses via its raised blood sugar levels and the need to replenish the post-adrenalin rush due to this unexpected interruption. It was a little 'Heath Robinson,' but it was all that I had, so I was rolling with it.

It was a minor victory at best, but I couldn't afford the luxury of time to self-admire.

Whilst they were busy answering them, I reported the incident and began the search for a new room.

They were momentarily rooted to the spot as once again they heard words that would never emerge from my mouth.

"Five-minute break everyone, quickly clean yourselves up and refocus for the second half of the lesson. On your return, the new room number will be on a post-it note on the back of this door."

"Is she alright?"

They were not going to wait for me to change my mind and swiftly raced for the door.

I noted a nod to my colleague, followed by a whisper,

"Ta for this, you can come again."

The lesson resumed and the class had settled down. My colleague remained for an additional 15 minutes.

'The feedback will be interesting.'

As luck would have it, the lesson appeared to have been a relative success. Much to my amazement, my colleague verbalised that she would have struggled to handle the situation. She remarked on my creativity and admired my tenacity.

I could now afford to reward myself with a small smile. I still have no idea why or how I handled it as I did.

I often wondered about that day and how dangerous it might have been to remain in the room.

Was there mercury in the air? Who knows.

FAILING TO IMPRESS

A brief introduction to Kevin

Kevin was tall. In fact, he was very tall and held that typical self-assured stance held by people of a similar ilk; that was to stand with his legs apart, often with his arms folded, whilst holding a conversation. To my knowledge, he had never been absent from work in the ten years that we had been working together. He didn't like change. Kitted out in his shorts and fleece, he would often be waiting at the college doors for the caretaking staff to open the building up. The weather conditions failed to change his mode of attire. He could be found firmly ensconced in the P.E. office happily relishing his solitude.

He was approachable and had a work ethic to be admired by all, including the senior management team. When told that the newly installed smart boards were to be used by all staff, with training imminent, he protested and asked for and received his own overhead projector (OHP). Wherever Kevin was, the OHP was too, within striking distance. From time to time, he could be seen wheeling a TV on a trolley towards his classroom.

He eventually had to succumb to the technology wheel before it ran him over.

Having now retired, Kevin recalled the onset of his career with a sigh. Being a new teacher is tough. There's a constant stream of people looking over your shoulder, checking and cross-checking all aspects of your work. You are on tenterhooks as you double and treble check all the accoutrements needed for the day; including changes of outfits as you run from practical to theory lesson whilst also ensuring that you have the correct array of equipment for each lesson.

If you teach Physical Education, there's always the tricky changing room situation to manage. Perhaps it's the intermingling of fresh or not-so-fresh bodies in various phases of undress and the shyness or boldness of the boys, due to their levels of physical maturation for example. It was a miracle there were no daily occurrences of unintentional clothes swaps due to the proximity of the clothes pegs.

The changing rooms were designed to hold a maximum of thirty pupils at one time. This day though, classes had to be doubled up. The sixty boys swiftly became acquainted with each other's' bodies, in a manner not of their choosing. They were crammed between the benches, walls, and clothes pegs. Despite the closeness of their proximity, issues were kept to a minimum due to the organisational skills of the staff. This lesson was completed with little incident and the boys changed in preparation for their next period. The teachers were busy in their office sorting out borrowed kit whilst preparing for the next lesson. Kevin dismissed the class from his office door. They all dutifully left except for one little boy. A quiet knock on the door interrupted the staff. Kevin, 6′ 4″ on a good day, looked out and saw no one, then, looking down, he saw Peter. There were tears in his eyes.

With a nod of his head, Kevin reassured Peter and gave him time to compose himself.

"Sir, I haven't got both of my trainers, but I've got these."

He held up a pair of training shoes, not so much a matching pair, but two individual items of footwear. Peter looked down towards his feet whilst simultaneously rocking back and forth. Kevin mentally made note of this boy's predicament; in one hand was a brown trainer and in his other, a black one. On second viewing, he noted not only was this poor child holding up odd-coloured trainers but in addition, one had laces, and the other had Velcro tape. Someone had taken the wrong footwear. How was this possible? Surely the other child would have noticed, unless this was a prank.

The poor child was told to remain where he was whilst the possible prankster was apprehended. The Head of the Department agreed to hold the fort, manage the incoming class whilst simultaneously keeping an eye on the increasingly distressed Peter and his mismatching footwear.

Kevin quickly made his way to the admin office to review the timetables and the boys' next locations. The school bell had just been rung, so the pupils were making their way to their lessons. He climbed the stairs two at a time in an attempt to intercept the class therefore minimising any disruption. He explained his predicament to the teacher at the classroom door and waited until the pupils were allowed inside. The register was taken to ensure that all were present before he scoured the room looking at the boys' feet. No explanation was given to the class as they curiously watched him in action. He thanked the teacher and exited the class empty-handed. He quickly made his way across the building to the next class, repeating his explanation to the member of staff whilst his eyes hurriedly searched below the desks. These actions emitted a strange combination of curiosity and embarrassment once more as their eyes followed him around the class. He spotted the culprit.

It was James.

He whispered in his ear and asked to see him outside. The poor boy seemed a little alarmed; Kevin placed a reassuring arm on his shoulder and escorted him out of the room, thanking the teacher with a nod.

The door closed, Kevin looked down and knelt to match James' height. He immediately knew that something wasn't quite right. The poor boy hadn't registered that anything was amiss. Kevin proceeded to look down towards the boy's feet. Having tracked Kevin's eyes, he followed suit and he too noted his footwear.

"Oops."

Was the only sound he managed to utter.

At that juncture, Kevin came to the realisation that scolding James would be futile. Instead, he guided him back to the changing room to facilitate the exchange. His exasperation was so profound that the idea of discussing the oversight of wearing mismatched footwear, with the two distinct fastenings, seemed beyond consideration.

The blissful obliviousness of those boys.

WHAT HE DOESN'T KNOW WON'T HURT HIM

A brief introduction to Donovan

Donovan was shorter than the average British male and made up for this by the length of his stride. His cadence carried with it an inbuilt sense of pride and purpose and he walked with a sense of self-assurance of his status within the college. He was well-read and liked to debate on the latest political topics. As a member of the senior management team, he held a lot of power. He was often seen holding court with staff and students alike, deep in conversation, exercising his brain cells. In other words, he could talk. Geography was his perfect sounding board.

The lesson began as normal. There was the usual small talk as Donovan unlocked the door and opened it just enough for his students to squeeze through into the classroom in single file. He strode over to the whiteboard, reached for the remote control, and pressed the switch that brought the projector to life. He then turned his attention towards the computer, switched that on too and found the PowerPoint for the lesson. He explained the lesson starter, claiming that the work will soon be displayed on the screen. His eyes glanced towards his desk, and he let out an audible sigh. He turned to the class and stated that he needed to collect the handouts for the lesson. He exited the room. Rob, probably one of the most unassumingly quiet students, decided to do something a little unusual that day. He removed the bandana that held his curly blond locks in place, stood on a table and tied it around the projector, blanking out the screen.

The classroom door is designed to open in such a manner, that upon entering the room, the person entering is instantly faced with its occupants; this also partially obscured the wall housing the whiteboard. As Donovan re-entered the room, the class was aware that they were powerless to revise their non-working status. He instantly realised that the students had not been using their time as he would have wished. He abruptly halted his stride and a look of both confusion and annoyance crossed his face. He turned to face the direction of the computer at the far side of the class and made purposeful strides towards it. He began to express his disappointment at the lack of dedication to their studies and was halted mid-sentence as, to his dismay, it was then that he observed the blank whiteboard. His head dipped and he slowly turned as he realised that the projector had failed to display his PowerPoint. Without a cursory glance at the projector, and trying to ignore everything around him, he placed himself in front of the computer and tried in vain to work out what had gone wrong. He turned it off, then back on, checked the mouse and the wiring to see if there were any loose connections, there was no progress to be made. Eventually, he gave up, and having admitted defeat, he went to summon help from the IT technicians. Not a sound was uttered from any of the students, no voicing of any concern, no offers of help and most interestingly of all, there were no giggles. They just sat and smirked whenever he turned his head away from their line of sight.

Rob, suddenly overcome with guilt, realised that maybe he might have gone a little too far. It was time to remove the bandana from its new home. The technician he surmised, would spot it instantly, then who knows what would happen to him. He swiftly reversed his actions from earlier in the lesson. With his bandana in place, and his hair once more under control he took his seat. A visibly frustrated Donovan re-entered the room with the technician close at hand.

Rob exclaimed,

"Look, Donovan, it's workin'. We managed to fix it."

Donovan had of course tried everything in his power to fix the issue and asked how they had managed it.

"We found another wire that wer' loose. We put it back in and it's fine naw."

He examined Rob's innocent face and saw no purpose in pursuing the point any further.

It has been said that confession is good for the soul. Is this still relevant 15 years later?

A LITTLE TOO CRUEL?

A brief introduction to Rob

Rob was the salt of the earth type of young man, a bit of a homeboy as he had not ventured too far from his place of birth. He was tall, affable, loved cricket, was trustworthy and held a head full of blond curls, not too dissimilar to the child actor Shirley Temple. This added to his 'butter wouldn't melt in his mouth' look. You could rely on him for almost anything. He was the go-to student who could be counted on when the class struggled to answer questions.

During one Christmas period, the tree was taken out of its usual hiding place on the third floor and lovingly decorated by the admin staff. The festive theme was complete when the beautifully wrapped presents were residing at its base. The tree was on full display for all to see as they descended the steps from the two sides of the college building. The presents were just empty boxes, but they served their purpose.

Christmas is the season for giving, so the geography class, led by Rob, thought that it would be a good idea to provide their teacher, Donovan, with a present this year.

The present of course originated from under the colleges' tree. At the onset of the lesson, Rob, the self-appointed class spokesperson, addressed Donovan with a short speech of gratitude whilst simultaneously handing over the present. A bout of shyness had suddenly crept up on him. His head lowered as he swiftly took his seat. Donovan bless him, was overjoyed with the generosity of his students, stating how thoughtful it was of them to think of him. The students muttered refrains of,

"It was nothing."

"It wer' nowt."

He refused to shake the box or ask about its content. Instead, he said the unexpected and announced that as they had so kindly bought him a present, it would be an injustice to hold it until Christmas. He would therefore open the present there and then. The students braced themselves.

This was not in the plan.

He eagerly tore the wrapping and proceeded to open the box. He was speechless. He peered inside. his eyes searched every corner and came up with nothing.

It was empty.

Silence followed.

Rob didn't exactly own up to the prank but voiced how the class had overheard Donovan stating that he was always up for a laugh as his position as vice principal usually entailed serious matters. Donovan was left with no choice but to express the ingenuity of the caper and how he managed to fall for it. No harm was done. Or at least those words were voiced. The students' responses were a little muted.

Donovan steeled himself and continued with his planned lesson. There was nothing to be said that would improve the situation.

After 15 years, Rob felt that it was the right time to unburden himself. He and Donovan were now working in the same institution so maybe he would see the humour in it all.

He confessed only to me in the hope that Donovan would read this chapter and that together, as adults, they would work it out.

JUST SHOOTING THE BREEZE WITH A FEW CONFESSIONS

Rashawn and Elijah are now young men in their early thirties. We arranged to meet in 2021 to reminisce upon our time together at the sixth form college.

Rashawn's Confession

In the early days of the college, there were very few sports facilities on-site. In fact, due to the size of the site, the situation has remained the same to this day. We hired the practical facilities from the prestigious English Institute of Sport, with the view to attracting potential sports students. The hope was not only to inspire students with the facilities and surroundings but also to provide a vicarious learning experience as the students observed the lives and expertise of the athletes and their coaches. In our efforts to maintain a professional outlook, we also rented a classroom, where we taught at the institute for either a full or half-day. One of the main advantages was the opportunity to sit and soak up the atmosphere as the coaches and athletes went about their routines. Our allocated classroom and changing rooms were situated towards the opposing ends of the building.

The students had completed their theory lesson and were due to begin their practical session in the sports hall. Heather was still in the classroom making last-minute changes to her planning. Rashawn rushed up the stairs, ran the length of the corridor and burst into the room. He attempted to collect himself and grappled with the most appropriate language that he needed to use to convey his announcement. Nothing came to mind. From his mouth poured,

"Ahh, you need to come quick! He's pooing himself."

The effect was prompt. Heather sprang into action and bounded towards the classroom exit. Her hands instantly gripped the door frame, leaving her upper body protruding out of the door at a jaunty V-shaped angle. Her feet refused to move any further. She maintained this position whilst looking frantically in all directions.

"Where is he?"

Rashawn, maintaining his look of concern, pointed towards the stands surrounding the volleyball courts.

"He's gone down there."

Poor Heather appeared to be in shock and for once was at a loss for any sensible response. Her eyes widened whilst they rotated in their sockets searching for who knows what.

One by one a few of the class rushed up the stairs to support Rashawn's story. They were keen to embellish the story further and were equally keen to maintain a safe distance from Heather should the prank collapse.

"Well, he needs to get changed, doesn't he?"

Was all that she could utter.

This made no sense to the situation that she found herself in. Nothing else had come to mind.

Her reluctance to travel further than the exterior of the doors to investigate might have signified that she was still trying to process the matter of having to deal with biological waste products. Secretly, she was hoping that the situation would resolve itself without her intervention.

Whilst she remained locked between the class and hallway, questions constantly flew from Heather's mouth. The students couldn't hold it together any longer and eventually broke down. Initially, a head bowed, swiftly followed by a snort, then came the increasingly reddened faces, shoulder shaking and then finally the apologies flowed. An audible sigh of relief escaped her mouth, promptly followed by a mild chastisement.

In the back of her mind, she knew that she still had her secret weapon; they still had their practical session to get through. The gloves were now off. Heather began to make some vital tweaks to her warm-up session, somehow the students were not going to forget this day in a hurry.

***

The college had two lifts situated on either side of its small building; students were allowed to travel in them if they had a disability, injury or illness that prevented them from walking up the main sets of stairs. Access cards had to be applied for in advance and then picked up from reception, or staff would occasionally lend their card passes to students if they were helping with equipment transportation.

None of these scenarios ever happened to Elijah. He displayed a level of rude health. There was never a day of absence from ill health throughout his three years in college. He would inevitably be late for each of his lessons, even those in the middle of the day. It was highly unlikely that a member of staff would ever loan him their card. Yet his confession still did not surprise me.

"I had hold of one of those key cards for a bit."

My immediate response was,

"How did you get that then?"

They laughed Instantaneously. It seemed to be tinged with a little guilt.

Rashawn leapt to his friend's defence.

"We did, didn't we? Probably when Ben broke his leg, so we got a free ride."

They were a little hazy on exactly how they managed to possess the key card but surmised that Ben might have 'accidentally' lost his and was reallocated another.

Some conversations should not be pursued.

****

Elijah had developed the knack for attracting girls. All girls. His mere presence in any area of the college would bring them flocking towards him. It didn't matter where he was, but you could imagine the testosterone trail emanating from his body reaching out towards any unsuspecting girl and dragging her towards him. This often proved to be a little distracting when trying to teach him. The frequent classroom disruptions would be peppered with excuses from impressionable girls who would do anything just to get him to look in their general direction. Elijah and Rashawn helped to encourage the situation when they decided to implement the 'carry my jacket for the day' system for the young women in their pursuit. They would politely knock on my classroom door when the lesson was in full flow and sheepishly ask if they could return the boys' jackets.

The English Institute of Sport had its attractions but there were a few unexpected issues that occasionally occurred and needed to be handled delicately. The students would regularly support the local and regional school sporting events as Marshalls or other officials. From this, they would gain invaluable experience working with the public and young children and gain a few officiating and academic qualifications.

On one such occasion, the young men were sitting in the stands during one of their rest periods. A few supportive parents were there. One of the mums appeared to have fallen under the 'Elijah spell,' and somehow found herself gravitating towards him. She then managed to place herself next to him, asking multiple inconsequential questions that could have been answered by any of the participants or their teachers. Elijah and Rashawn exchanged wry smiles. Elijah subconsciously turned on his charm offensive, looked straight into her eyes, answered her questions and politely excused himself each time he was needed on the athletics track. Every break, as if by magic, she arrived at his side. Elijah, ever the young gentleman, was keen to comply and provided just the right amount of attention. This level of attention, unfortunately for her, was noted by Matthew, his teacher. He initially presumed that Elijah was informing a parent on the rudiments of the competition. As the afternoon continued, he observed the worrying regularity in which the presumed parent was at his student's side. As he observed the repeated conversations, he thought that either Elijah was finding it difficult to explain certain aspects clearly or something else could be developing. His mind didn't want to wander that far, especially as he was fully aware of Elijah's charm offensive. He continued to observe for a time, and when his mind once again began to take him to the worst-case scenarios, he made an executive decision to quickly whisk the young man away for additional duties, behind the scenes and out of sight from the public.

Whatever the situation was, it was instantly squashed. As disgruntled as Elijah was about this, he couldn't complain.

His charms had been successfully thwarted by his teacher.

***

The Education Maintenance Allowance (EMA) was a financial scheme given to students who were studying for at least twelve hours per week and whose households were under certain financial thresholds as set by the government. In a further attempt to keep them in education, they also had to comply with rules set by the educational establishments. If the students managed to comply with all of the rules, there were opportunities for bonuses at the end of the term too.

Elijah qualified for the EMA but rarely received his basic allowance due to his tardiness. He often tried to negotiate with me to change the late mark to one that indicated that he was on time. His negotiating skills improved, but his punctuality did not. Poor timing seemed to run through his veins. When it came to many aspects of his academic life, it just wasn't important enough to him; or, as he liked to phrase it, he had so many other important things to do each day that college work just got in the way.

The assignment hand-in days often brought along with it the usual flurry of,

"Can I have an extension?"

"No. But thanks for asking."

To Elijah, it brought genuine fear and alarm. Or was he blessed with extraordinary acting skills? The levels of surprise that he maintained throughout the years were Oscar worthy.

"When's that assignment due in?"

"Today."

"Today?"

The deadline days, as Elijah referred to them, would then find him missing other vital lessons to catch up on his work. He would sit in the furthest corner of the library with his fingers on fire as he ferociously tapped the keyboard to start and finish his work in one session. I used to walk slowly past the glass wall that separated the library from the main college corridor, knowing that he was residing there for the remainder of the day. On the odd occasion, I would walk inside and hear the tap, tap tapping of his keyboards as the volume and pace appeared to soar higher and faster than the collective body of students in the surrounding consoles. His grunts and groans would ricochet around the room as he tried his best to contain himself and hold the expletives in.

He continued with this method of assignment hand-in up until the last day of his final year. Everyone had completed their course and left the institution, yet here was Elijah in my office still working on his last few assignments.

On reflecting about those days, these were Rashawn and Elijah's thoughts:

"When you think about it, they weren't really that hard."

Elijah added:

"That wer' my problem, when I had to sit and do it, the grades were pass, merit and the highest grade were distinction. I knew exactly what I needed to do to pass each section. I wer' like, let's just do the passes first, then I'd look at the time, I might start the merit and then think, well it's done now init, it'll be alright. Now I sit and think that it hasn't made much difference, but I wish I had done it differently just for the discipline side of things. If I'd just got my discipline right, there and then ..."

He paused and sighed.

"I must have been so frustrating to have as a student."

I looked at him and with a wry smile, I thought to myself.

'If only you knew how frustrating and amusing you were in equal measures.'

He certainly kept me entertained though.

WHO'S SCHOOLING WHOM?

During the early days of the COVID-19 pandemic in 2020, and the first lockdown, I unexpectedly found myself with time on my hands. I was used to my days being busy from the time that I arose in the morning until the late evening. Suddenly, like much of the country, I wasn't travelling to and from work or working late to complete my lists of exponentially growing tasks. I couldn't attend my choir rehearsals, perform, or meet up with family, friends, and was unable to travel. This was replaced with online work, advising and comforting anxious staff and students alike regarding the issues that arose as a result of and throughout the pandemic.

We were all still ignorant of how to react to this new and as yet unnamed virus as we had never experienced a pandemic before. The rumours were rife; every surface area appeared to be riddled with it. This fed into the nation's ever-rising insecurities and proceeded to increase mine. I had time to stop, think and ponder about the fragilities of life and its temporary status. To maintain my sanity, I needed to change this mindset quickly. Nature was my anecdote. I'm a perpetual restless soul, always out and about, finding new activities to challenge my mind and body, so I decided that there was no time like the present than to explore my local area. It was Hobson's choice really; the word 'Lockdown' was self-explanatory. The one caveat was that we were allowed out of our homes once a day for daily exercise or restitution, and I was taking full advantage of this. My local park was becoming too congested, and despite being in the open air, the sheer weight of the throngs of people in it fed into my anxieties. The gyms were closed so exercising was to be completed within the local vicinity. The feeling of being hemmed in both inside and outside of my home just added to my rising levels of claustrophobia. The fear amongst the population in those days was palpable; no one knew exactly how the virus was spreading. Everything was being questioned.

I decided to walk along my local canal bank. The walk through the Victoria Quays never failed to capture my interest, it housed beautifully decorated boats and barges, and its alternative shops were full of peculiar objet d'art in its windows. Here, time was well spent; I could watch the boats being cleaned and repaired, admire the skeletons in contemplative repose on the barges at the canal front and just spend quality time reflecting. I often wondered if they were the real deal. It's a perfect spot for watching the world go by, escaping the crowds whilst viewing the rural and industrial backwaters of Sheffield.

On this particular walk, I found myself having to constantly clamber up the bank to give way to the oncoming traffic of people, or teeter along the water's edge to maintain a reasonable distance. My mind was constantly in overdrive; the idea of falling into the stagnant water resulting in hospitalisation did nothing to help my mental state, especially given the present climate. It occurred to me that other locals were becoming jaded with their neighbourhoods too and were also beginning to venture further afield, away from their usual haunts. So much for finding solitude. I made my way up the bank yet again for another cyclist. This masked cyclist though had approached and stopped in front of me, effectively blocking my path. I was a little perturbed, not knowing what to expect from this apparent confrontation. He quickly began to engage in conversation. At this point, I was a little taken aback as this person appeared unfamiliar to me. The mask and scarf were not doing me any favours.

We politely accepted each other's presence whilst he explained how he had been cycling for a few miles having taken his son out to the park. It was very busy, and he needed to find some solitude, so he had duly arrived here. We acknowledged the frustration in our present similar circumstances. Small talk aside, my mind was still churning as to whether I knew this person or whether he just felt the need to talk. My choices for movement were limited, he had already blocked my path and I couldn't reverse my direction of travel as he too was heading that way, thus defeating my idea of escape. I was effectively out of options.

"Already I've seen five people that I know."

He looked at me and seemed exasperated.

The penny dropped and I thought,

'I must be the sixth then.'

He wasn't just engaging in polite stranger conversation.

My mind was now in full swing trying to put the pieces together.

"Oh, congratulations on your son."

I was trying to buy myself more time. I reverted to my old tricks of attempting to fit together a possible academic year and the fellow students with whom he must have studied. Surely I must have taught him. I wasn't having much luck.

I vaguely remembered that I knew a few members of his family but there were no further developments as to who they were. Why was the mention of his son now beginning to feed my curiosity?

"You don't remember me, do you?"

No response came.

I busily searched his face, trying to glean some element of recognition, made increasingly difficult by his cycling accoutrements. I couldn't exactly ask him to remove them. Nothing was immediately forthcoming. We chatted about his family, university and how he was enjoying his studies. There comes a point in a conversation like this when I felt that the short window of opportunity had passed, and it was just too late to ask for his name. That time had now arrived. We said our goodbyes as time was pressing.

We continued on our separate ways, my mind then flew into overdrive trying to work out why I felt that he was no ordinary student. I'd congratulated him on his son. That was it. He had a son. His son... Why was this the sticking point? There was something peculiar about this.

It wasn't just one child, it was two! Nothing wrong with that. The saga swiftly unravelled in my mind…

He was the student that had to leave college promptly as fatherhood was quickly impending. It happened all of the time in college, but it wasn't one woman; he'd managed to get both of his girlfriends (or the two young women that he was seeing) pregnant at the same time. The boys were born within a week of each other.

Did the women know about each other?

How does that work?

Do the boys know of each other's existence?

How did he manage that situation?

His family were mostly from the church that I attended. Wow, how did he get through that baptism of fire? So many questions flew through my mind. I'd love to have been a fly on all of those walls. His mum and his uncles were all in church, some were ministerial leaders too. His life must have been hellish for quite some time.

Other thoughts then began to resurface; he had to leave college without completing his course. How did he get into university? As far as I know, he hadn't completed his studies. I remember him returning to college to ask my advice about higher education.

He was often humming tunes when working on tasks in the class, and I'd ask him about his musical tastes to see if I recognised any of them (and to see if I was still au fait with the latest genres). We'd often have a little banter about the origins of music, the artists and their inspirations, and whether the artists were plagiarising or paying homage to the original songwriters. One particular day, he was humming a tune that immediately took me back to my youth. I asked him about it. He stated with pride how great the riff and the beats were. It was Will Smith's 'Men in Black,' from the film of the same name. I stopped in my tracks,

'This student needs some schooling.'

I stopped the lesson, found the original song on my computer and then proceeded to play it to the class.

"This track was from my youth, I used to dance to this. It's Patrice Rushen's 'Forget Me Nots'."

"Aaah," he said. "Now I know why that's familiar, my mum's got this too."

That small comment put me right in my place. I'm not sure who was schooled then, him or me.

His innocent face just beamed right back at me.

BE CAREFUL WHAT YOU ASK FOR

A brief introduction to Michael

He wanted to complete his mortgage repayments by his fortieth birthday and didn't travel much. Well not as much as me anyway. He was friendly, popular with staff and students alike and was an open-toed sandal kind of guy. He was always willing to offer a helping hand, especially with IT issues. I'm speaking of myself again, but I'm sure that he was also generous to other staff too. He had a penchant for words, particularly complex ones.

Michael's Stories

When I was met with the typical student response of:

"But so-and-so-told me to!"

I almost always started with: "Are you a Myrmidon?"

This always throws the students off. When they asked its meaning I would say,

"Google it."

But they rarely had any idea of how to spell it! Sometimes I wondered if I was just being too cruel...but quickly changed my mind. I think not!

***

As teachers, we often wonder why some students attend college when they have absolutely no interest in their subject or even education for that matter. The answers are often complicated and can range from family pressure to having no choice, and many factors in between. As a result, a teacher's constant conundrum is what to do with these reluctant, often obstructive students.

Well, here's one method.

Michael recalled being utterly flummoxed by one such student in his lesson during his second week at the sixth form. His behaviour was shocking in the session and after countless gentle warnings of,

"I'd rather you didn't... please don't... that's inappropriate... he doesn't like you doing that to him."

He was eventually invited to leave.

"Are you throwing me out?"

"No, I'm not throwing you out, but I am inviting you to leave until you are ready to learn."

Here's where I pause, as every teacher knows whether you invite or tell a student to leave, this is where the power struggle can accelerate. Will they? Won't they? It can go several ways: some instantly back down; others take the opportunity to bait you and relish the invitation. A few bask in the attention and goad you to the point of escalation, feeling that they need to finish what they started. Backing down was not an option. Either way, this was always a worry as the class could sense 'a stand-off' developing. Work can pause or stop as students blatantly gawk and wait with bated breath to see who will be the first to concede defeat. There could have been a multitude of outcomes. Here's how this situation ended.

The invitation to leave, remained on the table. This went on for several minutes with him getting more and more vexed. He didn't accept the invitation until Michael simply turned to the rest of the class and offered them a fifteen-minute coffee break. Everyone, including Andy, the reluctant student, left the room. Michael had a plan, he removed Andy's name from a class email, informing them of a change of room for the second half of the lesson. He politely asked them not to notify Andy.

It had worked, the class reconvened in a new room. Andy arrived half an hour later, escorted by the principal. Michael invited Andy to explain what had happened. He seemed very unwilling to talk, but the rest of the class was very happy to fill in the gaps.

His behaviour improved dramatically after that episode. According to the class, Michael had 'owned him' with that trick. He still isn't exactly sure what 'owned' means in street language but took it as a compliment.

***

I have found over my many teaching years that the quality of the class alternates each year. There was always a range of behaviours and attitudes, but the spectrum can be from sublime to awful. This year the sports staff had hit the jackpot, we knew that we were going to have a glorious two years ahead of us.

These boys were a delight to teach from their first day; apart from my wardrobe malfunction (the delightful details are in my first book) their lips were uncharacteristically sealed for the next two years. The start of every lesson from that day forward was torturous as I continued to brace myself for the comments. I eventually learned to contain myself and bury my emotions.

What I really wanted them to do was to put me out of my misery or put me through it again and discuss the exposure incident once and for all. I was never going to be the one to draw their attention to it though. I just needed to get it out of the way and move on.

That never happened.

I taught this class a few times a week. Whenever they were required to complete online research and IT facilities were needed, Michael was my go-to person. He was usually obliging whenever I asked if I could share his room. It was in one of these lessons that his eyes were opened to the normal classroom behaviours of my boys. It's funny how things can be taken for granted until someone brings them to your attention. This was one such occasion.

It was midway through their first year and the class had bonded extremely well; probably too well. The first five minutes of every lesson was always taken up with mutual boy-on -boy compliments. There was one sole female in the class; she was always ignored. The boys would preen each other, cuddle, sag into each other's arms for comfort and reassurance, comb each other's hair, spray one another, stand back and make announcements regarding their peer's wonderful qualities as if they were to be awarded prizes in oratory. I was constantly telling them to refrain from hanging off each other's necks and to complete their work. It was during one such lesson that I acknowledged the alarm on Michael's face when witnessing such behaviour. To reassure him that this was normal practice, I stated that they were so protective of each other that when taking part in practical sports sessions, they would never fully commit to any interactive skills. The fear of hurting each other far outweighed the significance of the sport or their grades. When this occasionally happened, everyone, except my female student, would pause the lesson, fawn over the injured player, check that there was no permanent damage, whilst ensuring that their hair was just right, and designer trainers unmarked!

***

There were always a few students who failed to listen to any advice given to them. They appeared to be hellbent on driving the teachers and their students to distraction. Methods to combat this behaviour would be chosen, then immediately discarded as they failed time and time again.

These students were often present in body, but vacant in mind; they were non-participators, yet expected the highest grades even when their work is often last minute and incomplete.

One such student, Nathan, took this to the nth degree. He was at the front of the queue in terms of non-completion of any group work or tasks both in and out of the classroom. Eventually, his teachers stopped trying to cajole him into working and saved their energies for the students who wanted and needed them. This was not the best teaching philosophy, but sometimes our sanity needed to be preserved. Nathan, to coin a phrase, was never boring. Somehow, he made it through to the end of his first year and onto the second year of his course by way of a formal Disciplinary Panel. He made the usual promises to complete his outstanding units over the summer. Was I doubting Nathan here? Well, if he couldn't work in term time with support, what on earth was going to make him give up his free summer?

Nothing, that's what.

The summer came and went, and I'm sure Nathan had a great time. Enrolment time arrived, and so too had the date for his completed work to be handed in. Nathan arrived empty-handed.

During enrolment, the college placed stickers on students' files where there were a number of issues in their previous year, indicating that a conversation with a manager was needed. A decision was then made on their academic future. Nathan's file was no exception. He was duly asked to wait until he could be seen. This is where it went a little awry, or 'Pete Tong', as the saying goes.

Several staff meetings were held at the onset of the academic year to ensure that all members of staff were thoroughly briefed on the enrolment procedures. Where they were not, they were buddied up with a more experienced member of staff to safely guide them through the process. Every morning of the enrolment week, the rules were reiterated with a series of bullet points from the principal.

- Students should not, under any circumstances be handed their files.
- The folders often held very sensitive information from their previous establishments or their previous year of study.
- Should they happen to uncover any of this, it could cause lasting damage.

Nathan was handed his file.

He was placed on a seat to await further instructions.

He sat with his file on his lap and noted the sticker and notes attached to the front.

Opportunity one.

He ripped off the sticker and casually joined the line of new students waiting to enrol.

Opportunity two.

Whilst in the queue, Nathan casually scrutinised the plaza area to identify his subject teachers, placed himself in another queue to avoid them, and managed to re-enrol himself seamlessly onto the second year of his course. This blunder remained undetected throughout the whole enrolment procedure, until his bottom was firmly placed on his favourite chair amongst his peers for his first lesson. He must have been giddy with his little triumph. His teachers were baffled as to how he managed to wangle his way onto his second year. Did he learn his lesson? Oh no, he felt that he had the gods on his side.

He was now safely ensconced onto the latter half of his course. The protests from the staff, although armed with evidence from his previous year, could not progress any further. Nathan had, after all, followed the rules on the day, and completed all the correct legal documents during his enrolment; these in turn were signed by members of staff who were oblivious to his situation. So, although attempts were made to contest the decision, this could not be taken further without disciplinary procedures against the college. We couldn't afford the media attention.

During the first term of the college year, he completed his university application. He had been successful so far, why change the habits of a lifetime?

The teachers persevered and cajoled him for a little while to no avail. For his part, he continued to ignore them and worked solely on the units that he enjoyed the most. The end of the year arrived, and the staff had one last trick up their sleeves: they could lock the units online. This act would prevent anyone from uploading grades onto the system after the identified closing date. They were only working to college rules after all. Through his own volition, Nathan would then have an incomplete grade profile; in due course, his chosen university would then receive his course grades. These would be insufficient for his course of choice. He would therefore be unable to attend his chosen university. Or so we thought.

The following September arrived; Nathan strolled into the university buildings towards the administration's officer. He was asked for his results certificate.

"Oh, yes, I've posted them to you, didn't you receive them? I've passed my course."

He was politely asked to return to college for a copy of his results as they were not on the system.

In the middle of September, in what should have been his first year at university, Nathan arrived at college and politely knocked on the principal's door. He had a complaint against the staff from his previous year. He claimed that they had been against him for much of his college life and had refused to help him. They had deliberately failed him on some of his units. He went on to explain that he should have gained additional grades for some of his work, but the staff had denied him his rights and so are now preventing him from pursuing the career that he rightly deserved. He wanted this to be formally investigated. She listened, nodded, and noted his comments. She picked up the phone and talked to John, the Head of the curriculum area. She thanked Nathan for his information and directed him down the corridor to John's office. John, in turn, listened intently to his story and mentally filed the information regarding his unit failures, lost opportunities, and the low grades awarded to Nathan by his teaching team. He too picked up the phone and spoke to Michael who had taught him for much of the year. He asked him if he could see Nathan's work files for the last two years.

After two years of study, most students would have been able to stake a claim for reforesting plantations with the amount of paper documentation that they had produced.

Such is the extent of the weight of the work produced by them at the end of their course, that upon collection, they often needed reinforced bags to carry their bulging two A4 folders home with them; IT students were not exempt from this.

After a little time, Michael ceremoniously walked into John's office carrying Nathan's folder as though he was the ring bearer at a wedding. A single A4 folder was presented to them, neat, untouched, and very clean. He extended his hands towards John and transferred the work over. John acknowledged the ceremonious passing of the folder. He then sat down and opened up the course spreadsheet on his computer. He liked data, it told him everything that he needed to know about a student, and the staff for that matter. He kept Nathan waiting. After an hour or so, as he looked at the grades online and cross-checked them with Nathan's marked work in his folder, he finally made an announcement.

"I agree with Michael. According to the evidence on the spreadsheet and that of your folder, the staff have marked your work accurately. In fact, at some points, they may even have been a little too generous. I would have awarded you far less. They can't be changed as they have been reported to the board.

The moral of the story Nathan, is that grades can go down as well as up. You can take your protest further and appeal to the exam board. Should you choose to do so, I will be recommending that with the evidence presented, that a few of your marks are downgraded."

With that, Nathan silently shuffled out of John's office leaving the door ajar.

WHO'D BE A SUPPLY TEACHER?

A brief introduction to Katy

Katy was a newly qualified teacher; she had been working in different schools as a supply teacher until she found herself a suitable permanent post. She was a social butterfly and an effervescent character. At times her over enthusiasm needed a little reigning in, especially in the mornings. Or it could have been possible that I needed to be more awake in the mornings and open to conversations.

As a cover teacher, positions are often accepted at the last minute. Phone calls can be received early in the morning, requiring an immediate response. You never know what type of institution that you're going to be placed in, the subject to be taught, or of equal importance, who you're going to be teaching. You're filled with equal measures of excitement and dread. The excitement of the fact that you'll be teaching again, and getting paid, the dread of not knowing who the students are. What condition did the teacher leave them in? What condition was the absent teacher in? Was it stress related? Illness? Both? The mind can often travel to dark places when stepping into the void.

Today it was a class of 13–14-year-olds. Sometimes you're able to set out your stall in advance. In other words, set up, prepare, and wait for the class. Today was not one of those days. Katy entered the room. Everything seemed normal, she looked at the whiteboard. Today's lesson was French.

'A walk in the park,' Katy thought.

The children were already in the class. Katy looked at the teacher's notes and became aware that a girl was trying to make eye contact with her. She was using sign language. She had signalled for Katy to meet her in the corridor. Eager to please, Katy set the class a starter task before she began the discussion with the as-yet-unnamed pupil. She opened the door and stepped into the corridor with the girl following closely behind. As they did so, the girl began to laugh. Katy was taken by surprise as she presumed that the girl was unable to speak.

'Maybe she signs for a relative or friend,' she thought, but didn't bother to ask.

With their conversation at an end, Katy returned to her class.

No one was there.

Not a single person.

No one had passed her in the corridor. Katy paused. Her eyes fixated on an open window. A thought had crossed her mind, but the class was on the third floor.

With her heart in her mouth, she began to panic. This was madness, there's no way that they could all jump out. Was there a door that she was unaware of? No. There's one way in and one way out. The panic rose from her gut and stuck in her throat; she felt the acid burn. With her heart pounding her eyes began to fill with tears. In a fit of pique, she ran towards the windows, not knowing what she would find. She looked out and noticed a drainpipe next to it and could only come to one conclusion.

They had all escaped down it.

What other explanation could there possibly be? Her eyes cast themselves downwards into the yard as she began to pick up on familiar noises. There they were, all running around screaming. She stared at them, momentarily incapacitated by the images below. Her mind was racing.

How/why did they do it? What am I going to do? This must be the class from hell. I don't know what to do. I'm in so much trouble.

She paused, composed herself and exhaled.

'They got themselves down there, they can get themselves back up.'

With that decision made, her mood improved, then came the self-doubt.

'How exactly am I going to do this?'

They didn't know her, they held all the power, she just had to reclaim it. Thoughts raced through her mind. Shimmying down a drainpipe is relatively easy if a little tricky. Gravity and a little strength help. What were her options? None, she felt. She had no alternative but to lean out of the window. In her most authoritative teacher voice, she ordered them to return to the classroom at once, whilst simultaneously pointing towards the doors. Her voice projection had worked, and she allowed herself a small triumphant smile as the class froze to the spot and looked up at her. She pointed towards the entrance door again and proceeded to watch for any additional escapees. They reluctantly meandered towards the door. Katy continued to monitor the scene but noticed after a while that a crowd had built up at the door entrance. To her alarm she noted that the children in front were being squashed. She shouted again, to gently encourage them of course, and was also greatly aware of not drawing too much attention to her plight... probably a little late at this time. A pupil looked up at her, bad timing on his part. They locked eyes; Katy drew him in. No words escaped from her lips, but he was compelled to explain the situation. He whimpered, "Between lessons all of the doors on the ground floor were locked."

"The doors were what? Locked? Is this a prison or a school?"

There was no time for semantics now though; she parked those thoughts in the back of her mind for later. Her predicament had remained unchanged. She eyeballed the pipe to her left. No choice then, they'll have to re-enter the room the way they exited. Up the drainpipe. There was still the issue of the classroom being on the third floor and the children being in the yard, on the ground floor.

'If only she could press the reverse button just for this duration...'

She could not afford such fanciful ideas and swiftly paused her thoughts. The whole idea of refilling the class with the children via their escape route was mind-bending enough. She followed this thought through and examined the drainpipe.

'How many times and to how many teachers had this class committed this outrage?'

She would bet her life that the Senior Management Team were aware if not fully cognisant of their antics.

The pipe looked sturdy enough, there were many sections where small hands could grip and sufficient brackets bolted into the walls for feet. She dug deep to recall her rock climbing lessons and the three points of contact needed for safety and began the retrieval process. Amazingly when shouted at yet again, the pupils complied. Much to her surprise, they obediently lined up beside the drainpipe. She wondered if they done this before?

'Should I get down there and help them?'

That thought was swiftly dismissed, the doors were locked. They had put themselves in this predicament, and she was unwilling to add herself to it. To be honest, she wasn't even sure if she could make her way down the drainpipe or if it could even hold her weight. She was just going to have to provide crystal clear verbal instructions and cross everything possible for luck. Let the ascent begin.

She watched curiously as they began to reshuffle the line around the pipe. Initially, she couldn't understand the processes behind this; she was also trying to visualise her instructions before repeating them to the class. She slowly began to instruct the first child on the climbing methods, initially fumbling over her words. The first pupil climbed up the pipe almost effortlessly. Katy swore under her breath and steadied herself, as she felt that her heart might jump out of her chest, she soon realised that this was almost a drill for them, her advice was peripheral to that of their peers. One by one in an organised fashion, they made their way up, unfazed with little fuss, and unscathed. This unsurprisingly took up most of the lesson time.

Once safely back in the class the adrenaline that had allowed Katy a modicum of control now almost brought her to a state of collapse. She downed tools. The teacher from the class next door was asked to enter the room, swiftly followed by another member of staff after complaints were made about the presence of children in the yard and shinning up the pipe. The staff leader, who was also the supply agency contact duly arrived too. Katy managed to hold herself together long enough to explain that she was unhappy (having chosen her words carefully). She continued her monologue stating that she had never witnessed this level of behaviour throughout all her years of teaching. A slight exaggeration of the truth she realised but they were not aware of that. She proceeded to relay the lesson to them as it unfolded, interjected with the behaviour management strategies that she had employed. She even supplied them with a review of how she saw that it had been orchestrated. Then came the question that she had been pondering,

'Had anything like this ever happened before?'

Unsurprisingly, it was revealed to her that three staff members were on long-term sick as a result of the class's behaviour. With that safely ensconced in her head, she politely asked them never to request her again. If this was the difference between working and not, she preferred to be unemployed. It was pure luck that no injuries had occurred. She forcefully stated that she would not be held responsible for their behaviours as it was clear that this had been embedded for some time. An apology was issued. On reflection, Katy is still unclear on its grounds, class behaviour, withholding essential information or both? Without any acknowledgement, Katy immediately left the building and advised them to find another muppet.

What happened to the pupil who initially diverted her attention? Who knows? She remained outside the class shouting to anyone who would listen:

"I'm not getting done."

TITS UP (DON'T JUDGE ME)

I'm flying through cover tutors like a hot knife through butter. They're either not staying as they can't cope with the occasional demanding student, or don't match up to our expectations. This one though might just last the distance. To be honest, I'm dead on my feet, or to coin my colleagues' phrase, 'teacher tired.'

The constant prepping and re-prepping of lessons, the inductions, reintroductions of new staff to students, and abandoning my classes to support the new staff, were beginning to take their toll on me and my team.

James, the latest in the line of supply teachers, had arrived. He was all smiley-faced in the morning, gushing about how much the students loved him and how they're so amenable to his style of teaching. This should have been music to my ears, but it wasn't. My suspicion radar had self-activated. I made a mental note to review the class activities and see how they were settling in with him, just to allay my suspicions. He sailed through all of the induction activities, and I presented him with the latest adjusted schemes of work and lesson plans, to which he seemed unfazed and remained quite enthusiastic.

It was the first lesson of the day, so I gave him time to settle the class and conduct the starter, as previously discussed. After twenty minutes or so, I slowly made my way up to the first floor where the lesson was being held. I could hear him before I could see him. There was a supporting wall on one side of the stairs, therefore obscuring the view to a few of the classrooms. We also had an open-door policy, so voices constantly travelled throughout the building, mixing and merging, often making interesting sentence combinations as you wandered from one area to another. I lingered and listened to the conversation taking place. James' voice had a particular tone to it. I immediately understood what he meant when he expressed the student's love for him. Well, when I mooted that a conversation was held, it was more of a monologue.

I slowly walked around the corner; the angle of approach still prevented the teacher from being seen if they were at the front of the class, but the students soon became aware of my presence and quickly changed gear. They were suddenly bending down and magicking their folders from their bags. Some even began to write notes, on what subject, I'm still unsure. I might not have been able to see the whole of James, but I could identify his lower half. He was not a small man, so couldn't manoeuvre himself quickly enough if he needed to.

There he was, well, part of him at least, at the end of the teacher's table. His feet were very comfortably positioned on the top of it with his soles facing toward the students. He continued to regale the students with his stories of sporting competitions and changing room banter and went on to offer them tickets that he was now selling for future basketball matches. There was no hint of my syllabus or lesson plan on his desk. He had failed to notice the sudden change in the student's demeanour, as they tried in vain to notify him of my presence. He continued unphased with his soliloquy. Suddenly, his disposition began to shift; he sat up and simultaneously slowly began to remove his feet from the desk. Speed was never going to be an issue here considering the size of his feet and girth. With his feet now firmly planted on terra firma, he swivelled his chair round to face the whiteboard, carefully supported his large frame with his arms, expelled a grunt and heaved himself out of his chair. His fingers clasped themselves around the nearest pen to hand. He stepped up to the board and immediately began to write. I didn't bother to check the script.

No words were exchanged.

'Mmm, that's not cutting it for me. We're going to have to have a few words.'

By that, I meant that I was going to have words with his agency. In reality Human Resources would have to deal with the matter. With that, I withdrew from the classroom entrance and climbed to the top floor towards the inevitable conversation with Michael in Human Resources. I began with an apology, that I was frustrated and then followed with my familiar phrase,

"He is not of the correct calibre; we can't work with him."

I went on to rant and spout about the dire situation that we were in. The ever-patient Michael sighed and told me to leave it with him. On receiving the delicately worded phone call, the agent was flummoxed. Struggling with a suitable reply he stated,

"Well, his references were so positive."

I was back to square one. Luckily for me, no further cover was necessary for Thursday. On Friday, the Chair of our Trust was holding his first all-academy trust training. This included our sixth form, along with the secondary, primary and infant schools. We were all meeting in the conference rooms of our local Premier League football club, so this was to be a huge event.

It was going as well as could be expected. During one of the breaks, Michael sidled up to me, looked at me and sheepishly stated,

"Err, a certain person is here."

"Is he?"

I knew exactly to whom he was referring. Annoyance was just one of the many emotions that raced through me at that point.

"I told him that he shouldn't be here as he finished on Wednesday."

I thanked him and mentioned that I would deal with it. I needed to be discreet about this; I didn't relish the additional attention that this could bring.

There was no sign of him anywhere until everyone was ushered into the main conference room for a plenary session. My eyes latched onto James as he was about to settle himself with a group. I could sense that he was about to launch into one of his soliloquies. I decided to save his unsuspecting audience from his well-versed 'sales patter' and quickly interjected and apologised to the group whilst ushering him into a corner. His eyes were firmly focused on me. I gave him no time to state his point of view. I faced up to him and began:

"You know it's training day and," I paused for effect, "this is purely for permanent members of staff. Thank you for coming but you won't be needed for this afternoon's session."

As I pointed to the door, he in turn pointed to a senior member of staff, declaring that he had asked her if he should be attending the training. His carefully framed question had omitted the vital factors of his present employment status with us, so she had answered in the affirmative. Should she have had all of the facts to hand, then her response would not have been the one that he had desired. By deduction, his plan had backfired. I remained firm and thanked him for his time. I remained at the exit and watched as he exited the building.

***

I'm back at square one. Louise, the new vice principal, had constantly shuffled and reshuffled timetables to fit the needs of the supply staff. My situation remained unchanged and there appeared to be no solution in sight. It was Groundhog Day yet again.

'Finally, this must be it.'

Michael had been sent a resume for a cover teacher from an agency, he duly forwarded it onto me. She sounded amazing.

'Where has she been all of these weeks?'

Enthused by this stroke of luck, I finally felt able to get the students and the team back on track. Michael had scrutinised her details; we all decided that she was a good fit.

Together, Louise, Michael, and I formed a rather over-enthusiastic welcome party in reception. This had to work. She approached the external gates before being buzzed into the building. Louise and Michael recognised her and immediately mouthed a simultaneous

"Oh no!"

I looked at them.

"Oh, no? What do you mean 'Oh no'? She's perfect, isn't she?"

Louise quickly interjected and addressed us.

"She's been here before. Last year, we had to inform her that the member of staff that she was covering had made such a remarkable improvement that she was returning to work earlier than expected. We had to tell a few porky pies as she was so ineffectual that it was better to be down a member of staff than have her cover for us. Now, she's here again. What are we going to do?"

I looked at them.

"What are *we* going to do? What are *you* going to do? This is not the remit of a Curriculum Manager, but human resources."

I turned to Michael.

"You can tell her goodbye. Now, what am I going to do? We'll have to start all over again and find someone else. I'll just go and teach two lessons at the same time. Just call me superwoman."

I didn't wait for a reply. We had all been heavily invested in finding a viable solution and were left exasperated over the situation.

I stepped back to watch them lead her into reception. I wanted no part of it. I watched her head bow as the news hit, then attempted to lip-read as the reality of the situation unfolded in front of her. To say she wasn't happy was an understatement. It was sometime before I dared to broach the subject of the details of the conversation. I had after all placed the ball firmly in their court.

THEY'RE MY SUPERPOWERS, I JUST CAN'T HELP IT

There are times when I wished that my sense of smell was not quite as acute as it was. It has landed me in some very tricky situations. I can detect a whole range of smells, from awful to exquisite. Unfortunately, I can also pinpoint with accuracy the owners of such bouquets.

I can detect the distinct differences in body smells arising from a whole gamut of situations, ranging from stress and anxiety, post-exercise sweat, freshly washed and unperfumed bodies, family smells and poor personal hygiene. I have even been known to follow unsuspecting people as at times, the smells that some people exude can send my pheromones into overdrive. So it's not all bad.

I'd catch myself holding my breath as I travelled up and down the stairs flanked by staff and students, often wondering why my chest hurt. I would frequently give my students a get out of jail free card when they entered my room by announcing,

"It's 9am, I'm not sure who owns that odour, but soap and water are free."

Not exactly true, but they understood my comment.

I knew exactly when that smell had arrived in the class, clinging to its owner. The students always looked around, trying to identify its origin, but I'd just leave the sentence hanging in the air. It's a tricky one to handle, as apart from the normal sensitivity surrounding the student, there can be many reasons for changes in smell. Often the fact that I had the windows open had little to do with my menopausal body, just that the invading concoctions of teenage body smells were sending my senses into overdrive.

My son's school friends knew of my reputation. On approaching our house, they'd slow down, lift their noses in the air to follow the imaginary smell wafting its way to my house and state,

"Mmm, Aaron's home. Who has he brought with him this time?"

THE WRONG FOOTWEAR

Wednesday had arrived, and with it my spinning class day. I enjoyed the effort and excessive amount of sweating that it produced, most of it stress-induced as I wasn't a natural performer on the bike. Well, I avoided the activity in public if I'm being honest. It just felt to be an uneasy partnership.

As my day consisted of juggling staff and student issues, the exercise helped me to expel the stress and anxiety that often threatened to overwhelm me. My bag as usual was packed and in the car. I hurried to the car park and set off with haste. I wanted my usual position in the class. I didn't want to appear too keen and neither did I relish the instructor constantly eyeballing me to keep up and increase my efforts.

I arrived in the changing room, bag in tow. Running late, I hastily found a locker and began to change and push my clothes into the awaiting space. A few women were happily chatting away, and I recognised one of the voices. We exchanged glances, nodded our acknowledgement of each other and proceeded to chat whilst I quickly continued to change. I then realised that she was the parent of one of my lovely students, Dan. He was struggling a little, so we were in regular contact to update her on his progress. She always appreciated the support.

I continued to get changed, grabbed one of the trainers out of my bag, and lifted my left foot onto the bench. I put on my sock, then proceeded to put my trainer on, job done. I lifted my other foot onto the bench, sock on, and picked up the other trainer before thinking,

'... mmm there's something not quite right here.'

The conversation resumed, but having glanced down at my left foot, I noticed that there was something a little odd. I then decided at this point that sitting might just be a good option. Why the change? I had a pair of trainers. Well, not a pair exactly, I had two trainers, but I'd discovered to my despair that they were both for my left foot. One navy blue, one black, they were different brands and on top of that, totally different heights.

'Surely this shouldn't make a difference though, I'm only on a bike after all,

In my rush that morning, I hadn't given a thought to what I was picking up. The subtlety of the design was previously lost on me. Now I noticed, how the curves neatly fitted the shape of each foot. Had Dan's mum noticed the shift in my demeanour? Or wondered why I suddenly needed to sit down? Either way, she hadn't vocalised her thoughts.

'What to do now?'

I needed to get to the class.

'How bad can it be?'

I proceeded to force my right foot into my unyielding left trainer. My toes resisted at every given stage, foretelling the torture that they were about to be put through. As I lifted the tongue of the trainer and eased my foot in, the fabric forced my big toe towards the right, leaving little room for the remaining four. This caused a scrunched-up layering effect. I continued to prod, poke and ease my foot into as reasonable a position as possible. With the task completed I sat back and emitted a satisfied sigh. Now, off to the class. I raised myself from the bench and immediately began to list towards the right. My right hip had dipped. The combination of scrunched-up toes, with an enforced swagger, must have made me a site to behold.

Not to be deterred, I mentally steadied myself and carefully proceeded to walk out of the door, with my head held high. With my listing gait, full focus was now needed to avoid unwanted attention in the footwear department.

There was to be no usual heel-toe repeat, I had to force my right foot to land purely on the ball of my foot, hoping to pull the walk off with aplomb.

My walk of shame had begun.

I arrived at my spin class drenched in sweat, not as a by-product of exercise but of anxiety. Luckily for me, everyone was still in the preparation mode of wiping down their bikes and were too engrossed in small talk to notice. I had spotted a vacant position, the second row in at the end, so I casually headed towards it. With the bike wiped down and the seat adjusted, I began to feel more settled.

'Drama over let's just get on with the class.'

I put my left foot into the stirrup and hoisted myself up onto the seat. The volume of the music increased to signal to the class that the instructor was ready to start. Then came the first set of instructions.

"OK, settle in and let's begin our steady climb up the mountain."

I placed my right foot into the stirrup, but it constantly slipped out. It wouldn't hold in either the up or the down phase. I soon identified the problem, it was the shape of my trainer, in fact, it was the excessive curve of this design that now firmly held my right foot. Yet again I hoped that I had not exposed myself to more unwanted attention. I must have looked as though I was having a seizure as I constantly listed off to the right only to quickly readjust. I just about managed to maintain my balance.

I concluded that if all else fails, fake it. Well, I'm sure we've all done that from time to time. My flustering and sweating escalated. I perfected the act of pulling my squashed toes towards the ceiling during the upwards phase, thereby actually causing me excessive cramping. On the downward phase with my extended leg, I pointed my toes down and inwards towards the bike frame. Just on my right foot. At the same time, I was trying to keep my left foot relaxed in cycling mode.

The concentration on my face must have been a picture. All because I didn't want anyone to see what an ass I was making of myself. Dan's mom was there too. Imagine her describing that story to her son.

Each time we were instructed to stand on our bikes and lean into the handlebars to pedal uphill ... well, put it like this, I didn't need the exercise to elevate my heart rate or open my pores more than they were already. I was sure that my heart was going to burst out of my chest, and I was leaking like a sieve. I leaned in and simulated increasing the resistance setting. That dial was going nowhere. There was no need to fake the increased effort at this point. The additional concentration required once my bottom had left the safety of the seat took every ounce of focus. I was constantly resisting my body's need to list to the right as I fought to remain in contact with the pedals. Was it worth it? Should I have given up? Maybe, but once I had made my decision and walked into the spin studio, I hadn't given myself any choice.

I collapsed in relief at the end, then excised my foot out of its ill-fitting footwear and hobbled down the corridor, leaving a sweaty trail in my wake. I didn't care about the impression that I was giving then. I finished the session having elevated my adrenalin levels, exceeded my target heart rate, and sweated an inordinate amount of moisture out of my body. All because at my base level, I'm a control freak. Did Dan's mom see or even care?

She never mentioned it.

THIS NEEDS TO STOP

I played competitive volleyball from my teenage years through to my mid-thirties. As it holds many technical components, it can be a little tricky to teach at times. The students, who were experts at everything, persistently pestered me to play a full game... even before they'd picked up their first ball. Against my better judgement, they eventually wore me down and I conceded to their relentless calls to play a match.

In one session, there were odd numbers, so I was asked to step in and play. I complied of course; it was my sport and also a chance to show off... just a little. I wanted to show them how it should be done. The game ambled along frustratingly as the students pretended to play statues on the court. To translate, they just didn't move towards the ball. In my best teacher voice, I continued to provide practical advice on the necessary movement skills throughout the session.

During the game, I vaguely remember the ball approaching me from diagonally across the court from my right side. A student was positioned in front of me. He was in the ideal position to receive the ball. At the last minute, he sidestepped, leaving me exposed. I instinctively dived onto the floor to retrieve the ball. I needed to have a word with myself.

'Do not repeat that action, you're out of practice, too old and oh my goodness, my breasts really hurt.'

Of course, these murmurings were all in my head. I brushed myself off and noted the admiration in the students' eyes. I nodded in recognition. The game meandered along in a similarly irritating fashion; their teamwork skills were minimal. The session was also being recorded as critical feedback was needed during the forthcoming weeks. A review of their movement skills always produced interesting conversations in conjunction with swift improvements. The students were also aware that video evidence was needed for the examination board.

After several rotations on the court, I found myself in the same position as before: at the back of the court to the left with the same student in front of me. We were receiving the service, and this time I was ready. I had quite long hair at the time and hadn't tied it up as I originally had no intention of participating. Tom, on the opposing team, had developed quite a good overarm serve and was keen to practice it. He served straight down the line towards Ben. At the last second, Ben decided that he couldn't receive the ball and just bent his head almost in deference to it. Of course, I hadn't noticed the motion until it was too late.

My face momentarily halted the ball's trajectory, forcing it in the opposite direction. It ricocheted off Ben's back and flew straight out of court. The silence was tangible. I froze, the pain made me want to scream.

"I'm OK,"

I muttered.

There came a vague mumbled apology from Ben. This went unanswered, I was too busy trying to hold myself together. Note to self again:

'This has got to stop.'

The students packed the equipment away.

"Do you want me to pack the camera away for you?"

'Shit, it's all been recorded.'

"Please."

The uneasy silence continued during the return trip to college on the minibus. With the camera firmly in my grip and with my face now beginning to throb, I made my way to my office, sat at my desk and turned on the computer. With the camera attached, I braced myself to re-live the pain and humiliation all over again. I ignored the skills section, focused on the game, held my breath and watched. The game unfolded before my eyes.

Due to the constant humming emanating from my face, I had temporarily erased the first incident from my mind. And then there it was, that dive. My shoulders curved in on themselves. I watched, involuntarily touched my chest, and winced as my breasts connected with the floor once more. After a brief pause, I refocused and continued to analyse the game. We rotated, I was in position five, to the left, at the back, and Ben in position four, left and front. I'd forgotten how tall he was. I watched Tom serve; Ben dipped his head. I was momentarily confused. I needed to review what I thought I saw. Ben's height had both saved me and resulted in the unfortunate ball contact. He was so tall that I couldn't see the ball's trajectory and hence didn't react. Equally, I could not be identified by the camera. There was just a small point to be made about my hair. The only evidence of being struck in the face was that of a shock of black hair springing into life and then rebounding to its original position as though I'd been electrocuted.

Ironically, Ben simultaneously became the author and the solution of my pain and embarrassment.

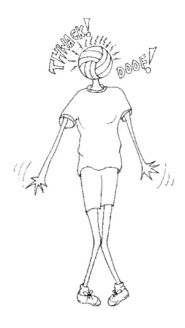

I WAS WARNED ABOUT JON

Each year, the British colleges held its annual national sports competition. To qualify for the finals residential weekend, each team or individual had to beat all of their competitors within their respective regions. This was the first year that I entered the competition with my male volleyball team. Much to my surprise, we took the regional trophy home. We then had the arduous task of raising funds and increasing the training schedule to give ourselves the best possible chance to lift the national trophy. In terms of sporting success, many of my college sports teams had also managed to win their regional competitions, so we had a large cohort of individuals and teams representing the Northeast UK region. For the first time, the college management acknowledged our success and rewarded us with a large donation towards the costs, alleviating the additional burden of having to raise substantial funds.

After the long journey, we were rewarded with a view of the beautiful surroundings. The setting couldn't have been more picturesque, all of the Northeastern Region were housed together in the beautiful historic buildings of Richmond's student halls of residence in South West

London. These were surrounded by acres of lush grounds that provided much-needed team bonding and vital chill-out time for the young athletes. My team was still riding high on the fact that they'd beaten the long-standing regional champions from Middlesbrough on their first attempt. Could they become national champions? Of course they could. I wanted them to dream big. I wanted them to work hard and let their hair down a little. Not too much though, I had my eye on the prize too.

The evening continued smoothly; meals were taken in the dining room with newly found friends. Being a little suspicious at how quickly some of the students latched onto their new compatriots, I made a mental note to complete a few rounds of the students' residences later that evening.

A few of the coaches had already made their way to the bars and looked to be firmly ensconced for the rest of the night. The sounds of the disco began to make its way through the grounds, enticing the students to lose their inhibitions on the dance floor. They were not allowed off the premises so had to make the best of the available entertainment on offer. I knew too well what that could mean, so decided to complete the first of my rounds early around the halls just to check on their welfare, so to speak. Upon entering the building, I noted a few students happily mingling in small groups, chatting along the length of the corridor. I held in my hands the room numbers of all my team, knowing that they would probably be huddled together in one room. I made my way along the corridor listening for any familiar voices whilst gently knocking on the doors. To my surprise I received a few replies, some of them had decided that they wanted an early night and had retired to bed. I wasn't convinced that much sleeping would be possible anytime soon as the level of noise was already irritating my ears. The additional concern was that a few of the hockey team were putting in some last-minute practice too. This could soon turn into a medical nightmare. A polite warning was therefore issued.

Further along the corridor, my ears tuned into a few familiar tones. The sounds of laughter resonated loudly through the door, straight to my ears. I neglected to knock as I had envisaged that the possibility of them responding to it was negligible. I casually opened the door and paused midway into the room.

I had been forewarned about Jon.

"He's trouble, you can't take him anywhere."

The details were sketchy as to what type of trouble this student brought with him. As far as I was concerned, from our history together, he had always been a hard worker and an invaluable team player. He had yet to disclose any of these troublesome qualities that were so freely spoken of.

Until today.

My sense of smell noted that there was something amiss in the air before my eyes latched onto the evidence. As I traced the origin of the aroma, there on the end of a hand was a large perfectly rolled spliff. Casting my eye further up the arm, I came across Jon's face.

It was smiling back at me.

I failed to return the gesture. I remained frozen for what seemed like an eternity. I scanned the room and noted the faces of my team; they were all looking in my direction. The room was silent. Mouths closed. I reversed my position and closed the door behind me. I misdirected my frustrations towards the hockey boys who continued to steadfastly perfect their drills. So, this was the trouble that they had hinted at. I now found myself in a conundrum.

'What do I do now?'

The boys had worked so hard, if I banned him from playing and we had an injury, that would mean the end of their competition. I decided to play the waiting game. I wasn't going to approach him and decided that he should come to me; we could work it out from there.

I didn't have long to wait.

When my back is against the wall, I try to regroup. I needed to go to one of my happy places, so retreated to the dance floor to work out my next move. As the Jamaican singer Shaggy's melodious tones sang out 'Mr. Bombastic,' Jon sidled up to me. I could feel the rest of the team watching from the side-lines, eager to interpret any type of visual display that might have emanated from us. I began to throw all kinds of dance shapes on the floor to buy myself more thinking time. Rumours later spread, remarking on how in-control I seemed to be for a drunken dancer. No drink had passed my lips. As the music developed, the crowd livened up, filling the air with the sounds of 'Shabba,' in time with the music. Jon apologised. The ice was broken. On reflection, he only apologised for being caught, not for smoking. He ended with,

"It won't happen again."

He was right.

It didn't.

In my response, I thought that it was my duty to reprimand him, not that it would have made any difference to his beliefs about his drug of choice. I could only appeal to his sense of duty, so I reminded him that as one of the older, more responsible students, he had a duty to behave more maturely when in the presence of minors. He in turn made the right type of gestures, indicating that he understood my point of view. I silently vowed never to put myself in that position again.

A few years later, Jon became my assistant coach when the girls also qualified for the national finals.

The evening came and went without further incident. The athletes and coaches all wandered off to their campus accommodation and I could finally celebrate having had only one small hiccup in the evening.

Later that evening whilst in bed, I heard a ringing noise inside my head.

'It's not my head, it's the fire alarm.'

I threw myself out of bed, casting a cursory glance down my body to check that I was reasonably dressed, and knocked on the doors in the corridor to get everyone out to the designated safe area. We assembled and heads were counted. All were present. It appeared to be a drill, so we waited patiently to be recalled to our buildings. We were finally waved forward and quickly returned to our rooms in the hope of catching up on our sleep.

The following morning at breakfast, sitting with the team, we reviewed the schedule for the day. They remarked on their broken sleep and the effects that the fire drill could have on their performance.

"What fire drill?"

Once more the team was silenced. In unison, they turned to look at Wayne, then slowly towards me. My mind was whirring and began to review last night's activities. I'm sure I knocked on his door and completed a head count.

'Whose head was I counting? How did I miss him? Why hadn't the team noticed his absence? Maybe I'd been drinking after all.'

Luckily for me, Wayne saw the funny side of it.

"It's alright, you can't get rid of me that easily. I'm your best player."

It could have gone so wrong but, with the tension broken, we laughed. Wayne was correct though; he was our best player in every position. To this day I still wonder how I had not noted his absence.

Over twenty years have passed, and I remain the firmest of friends with both Jon and Wayne.

ME AND SAMUEL L. JACKSON

On my desk and wall space were displayed the usual array of family photos and oddities. For most people, these supplied much-needed comfort, distraction and inspiration. Students often provided their unsolicited opinions when they identified my family members:

"Oh, you're married!"

"I didn't expect you to be married to someone like that!"

"Is that your son or your husband?"

I rarely replied.

There's one photograph that grabbed more attention than others though. A photograph of myself with the one and only Samuel L. Jackson. This took a central place of pride on my wall.

Not long after I had strategically placed the photo on my wall, a student walked in. He stopped and stared.

"Maxine," he paused. "Is that who I think it is? Is that Sam the Bad Man Jackson?"

He swiftly turned his face towards me, willing a positive reply from my lips.

I looked at him and gave him a knowing smile.

"How come you didn't drop his name before? Can you hook me up? Come on, you know I'm your favourite student. "

"I'll see what I can do."

I couldn't tell him that Sam was a waxwork image that I'd stood next to whilst having my photograph taken in New York.

He's still waiting for my reply.

WHAT'S IN A NAME?

There have been times when I've had multiple students with the same first and last names in the same class, often with slightly different spellings. A method had to be established that all parties agreed on, to help to differentiate between each person.

The principal held the same name as one of my students, it was a common name, so we were used to this. Unsurprisingly, the student never got used to the constant questions, accusations, insinuations, expectations and fear from fellow students and teachers alike, with everyone thinking that they were related. The idea that real or imagined close relatives co-exist within the same institution, can cause some young people to take extreme measures. A perfect example is that of my son, he decided to attend the same sixth form where I taught. He announced over breakfast one morning that he'd prefer to have a very early morning start and take the bus rather than be seen exiting from the same car as a member of staff, never mind the fact that his mother was also a member of the management team. The burden of having to arise from his bed at a ridiculously early time soon made him alter his ideas about his mode of transportation. A slight adjustment was made to his morning routine; he allowed me to drop him at the bottom of the road where he would then walk twenty minutes uphill. He rarely made eye contact with me around the building; only a handful of staff knew that we were related during his time there. He went to all that trouble, and we had slightly different last names too! Another colleague who was in the senior management team informed us that her daughter would be registered under her maiden name. Such is the fear of being recognised.

Imagine the sheer burden of being a student who possessed the same last name as the person who is the ruling authority of the institution. I was about to find out.

It wasn't pleasant. My email landed in the student's inbox, not the principal's. I'm sure that you can relate to the gamut of emotions that was experienced on discovering my blunder. The fast-developing knot in your stomach, the instant need to regurgitate recently eaten food or even the deep regret that is felt when the undo message pops up from your sent box and you wish you hadn't chosen to ignore it, or that you at least tried to view, check, change, retrieve or delete. That's what anyone with a modicum of IT knowledge should have done. That small hint should tell you that I held little knowledge in that department. Or knew how to do it if I'm being honest.

All of the aforementioned responses occurred when I happened to check my sent messages, something that I must do more often. My body immediately overheated, not too dissimilar to a serious menopausal flush. All was lost, or so I thought. My mind was racing,

'How could I solve this?'

Then that eureka moment presented itself. The IT technicians. I bolted from my office, ran down the stairs (always a dangerous pursuit), and knocked on the door. I walked in without waiting for a response and tried to remain calm and poised. The tech guys are always so nice to me and were constantly saving me from my IT dilemmas, so they were used to this. I felt the need to eat humble pie for this one though. I blurted out my problem and watched their faces as I realised that I appeared to be spewing out sets of incomprehensible phrases. I regrouped and rephrased to explain the extent of my error and to whom I had sent the email. I slipped in the fact that the content was confidential and asked,

"Is it possible to retrieve it?"

They took on a more serious tone,

"Well, it depends if the student has already opened the email."

That was not the answer that I was looking for. I visualised an Anne Boleyn moment with my head on the chopping block.

"You could also try going incognito to get into their account to check."

I feared that I was now losing the battle of keeping control of any of my bodily functions below the waistline. I had no idea what they were talking about. My ever-increasing levels of panic made the conversation even more of a foreign language than my usual scrambled affair. My body was sinking. Ryan, having witnessed my sudden slump, came to my rescue.

"Shall I come and talk you through it? That way you can make the changes yourself if this happens again."

I'd have done anything for him then... well, almost. Suffice it to say, I was overcome with gratitude and nearly hugged him. If you knew me, you would know that these emotional expressions are rare and reserved for very special occasions.

I learned an awful lot that afternoon. One interesting pointer was how to stalk or spy on people under the radar. I'll keep that up my sleeve for later as it could prove to be very handy. I was lucky, the email hadn't been opened and as Ryan could locate the student's password, we could easily delete the message without the student having an inkling that his email was being tampered with or as I would prefer to say, corrected.

Isn't hindsight wonderful? I can now sit and reflect on this close shave, one of many in my teaching life. I'm the product of my husband's IT expertise. When I have IT issues, his go-to phrase is,

"Pass it here, it's easier to do it myself than show you."

I used to take pleasure with that phrase, but now I'm not so sure.

"What does he mean when he says it's easier to do it myself?"

Well, that was one of those s**t nearly hitting the fan moments.

Another lesson learned.

Well, maybe.

PRIMARY SCHOOL INNOCENCE... OR IS IT?

I had an open-door policy where pupils could stay in the class during break or lunchtime should they ever feel the need to. One day, after playtime, I popped back into the class to prepare for my lesson. I noticed that Kevin was on his own. This often happened if one of the children needed some space or were a little upset. At first glance, he seemed to be OK. He was playing at his desk but appeared to be rather transfixed with his head facing downwards towards the floor. I then spotted the tip of a black object appearing and disappearing at regular intervals. The regularity of the as-yet-unknown object, coupled with the angle of Kevin's head and his concentrated face took my mind to a place where I didn't want it to go. My thoughts were in overdrive, and I fought to remain calm. Then I heard a noise proceeding from Kevin's direction; in fact, it was a steady throbbing sound that had suddenly caught the attention of my ears. I felt them twitch, I'm sure my whole body was at this point too. The idea that my supposedly innocent ten-year-old pupil was in my classroom on a self-discovery path doing heaven knows what with goodness knows what was unfathomable.

I slowly approached him whilst trying to feign as natural a conversation as possible, given the circumstances.

"Hey Kev, what have you got there?"

I was willing myself to remain calm and present, and not to jump the gun.

"Oh, it's just a torch, but I can't seem to get the light to turn on, it just keeps making this funny noise when I press the button. I think it needs fixing."

He twirled the object in his hand and passed it to me, whilst lifting his head towards me. His innocent eyes met mine as he willed me to help him.

My imagination wasn't being overactive at all, far from it. The evidence lay squarely in the palm of my hands vibrating away, all 30cm of it. It was of a dark hue, not too dissimilar from the colour of its recipient, hence my initial concern. My eyes scanned the object. To be honest, I couldn't move as I was transfixed. I noted with an increased sense of alarm how realistic it appeared to be. The level of detail was disturbing. It even looked uncircumcised. I continued to stare at it for what seemed like an inordinate amount of time when I felt a tug on my jumper.

"Sir, can you fix it?"

I immediately found the button and turned it off. My hand had begun to develop pins and needles. I now found myself in a similar stance to that of Kevin when I initially walked into the classroom.

"So, where did you find this?"

"In my mum's drawer in her bedroom."

"OK. Why were you in there?"

"I'd been looking for a torch all over the house and this was the only place that I could find one. I needed it to play in my tent."

He looked up at me, cocked his head to one side and smiled.

'Does he know? Is he waiting for a reaction from me?'

"Does your mum normally let you go through the drawers in her bedroom?"

I was only too aware of the pun as it exited my mouth but was helpless to stop it.

"No."

Came the coy reply.

Mmm, so he knew that he was in the wrong. I wondered, was he sheepish because of his discovery, searching his mum's bedroom drawers, or both? I didn't dare ask. He might have been more innocent than I was giving him credit for, and who was I to open up that can of worms? I decided to keep that lid firmly closed.

"OK, I'll keep hold of this for now."

This was all that I had managed to muster.

Unsurprisingly, I couldn't fully focus on my lesson after the break. I couldn't think of what to do with the contraption now lying silent in my desk drawer. A thought then occurred to me. It was lunchtime soon; all of the teachers would be in the staffroom. A little light relief was needed. I walked into the staffroom with the concealed implement. Everyone was engaged and fully focused on the usual challenges of the best and worst lesson, who was playing up as usual or who had made some surprising developments during the morning. The desk in the middle of the staffroom was usually full of dirty cups and half-prepared lunches. As good fortune would have it, it was surprisingly empty for the time of day, perfect for my unusual display. Eager to maintain the element of surprise, I turned my back to the staff, reached into my pocket, then placed the implement on the desk and pressed the button.

I stepped back and waited.

"I think that my story trumps all of yours, don't you?"

The conversations were immediately sucked out of the staffroom as ears pricked and everyone turned in unison towards the location of the sound. I swiftly scanned the room to capture the picture on their faces.

I pointed towards the implement.

"That's a torch, or so Kevin informed me. He was having trouble locating the light button and could only find the on switch. He seemed a little confused with it all and found it in his mum's bedroom drawer. I do believe, Miss Knight, that you have his class next."

I slowly turned to face her.

"I told him that I would hand it to you, and you would be happy to inform his mum that her torch had been found. I can imagine that she might be a little curious as to its whereabouts."

I didn't wait for any replies, not from Miss Knight or the other staff. I could see that they had remained as transfixed and lost for words as I had been earlier. By now, a few of the teachers turned to face Miss Knight with curious looks on their faces. I slowly retreated towards the door where I had entered incognito a little earlier. I knew that this had created such an unparalleled moment in the school's history that it would remain the subject of conversation for some time to come. Maybe a new protocol should be devised for such situations.

Coincidentally, parents' evening was fast approaching for this year group. The presence of Kevin's mum in the room facing Miss Knight would be enough to provide the evening's entertainment.

I couldn't wait, I wasn't the only one.

THAT SLIDING DOORS MOMENT

On the auspicious occasion of the wedding of one of my oldest friends, I decided to treat myself. I already had the perfect dress; it had been hanging unworn in the wardrobe for some time. The delayed wedding was just one of the many casualties of the COVID-19 pandemic. The total sum of my makeup amounted to a bottle of foundation, given to me around my sixtieth birthday, and two lipsticks, both similar shades of red. Yes, you read that correctly. My son constantly reminds me that I'm 'the least stereotypical woman ever.' As a result of this, at the age of thirty-two, he is still astounded at the amount of makeup and accessories that many of his past female partners possess. He, therefore, considers me to be a little freakish in terms of my attitude to these. The time had come for me to increase my lipstick range. I'm not sure if that constitutes a range but I'm claiming it. Whilst I was in the purchasing mood, I thought that I'd treat myself to a new pair of shoes too. My feet are huge and are always a source of trauma whenever people even mention feet in general conversation. In terms of stress, buying a pair of them is off the Richter Scale. The gravity of the occasion was not to be underestimated.

I found myself in a major Sheffield store two days before the wedding. Having spent a considerable amount of time with the shop assistant, much to her delight and my relief, I settled on a pair of shoes that were appropriate for the occasion with regards to the colour, style, and most importantly, fit. I quickly made my way to the checkout counter. I stood in the queue, masked and the appropriate distance away from the nearest customer in front of me. I waited patiently to be served. I noted that she had produced her store card from her purse. Ever the thrift-aware person, substitute that for cheapskate if you wish, I recalled that I too held such a card. Just not on my person. Never wanting to lose an opportunity to save money, when my time arrived to pay for my purchase, I speedily approached the cashier with my dilemma and wondered if there was any possibility of accessing my card number. She was to my surprise unphased by my issue and swiftly pointed in the direction of the accounts counter, where I would receive a day card. Having interpreted the gaze toward my purchase, she alleviated my concern by stating that my shoes would remain behind the counter awaiting my return.

I made my way up the elevator to accounts and was greeted by a small cheerful woman behind a protective Perspex screen. She proceeded to ask me to provide her with the usual details to find the correct card information. I complied and in turn she fed the details into the computer. She paused; looked at me and said,

"I don't mean to be rude, but did you used to be a teacher?"

This happened on a regular occurrence as I had been teaching for many years, so I wasn't too irked by the question. She paused again, exhaled, and said,

"Did you used to teach at H******* School?"

This time, I was the one to exhale. Usually, when I'm asked that teacher question, a process of elimination is mentally undertaken before I begin to respond. My usual train of thought is,

'Did we get on?'

As soon as that answer is secured, I try to frame the year and group of students or pupils that they knew or were associated with, to gain a better understanding of the person in front of me.

The fact that this mature woman had mentioned this school, immediately provided the time frame. This was from the autumn of 1983 to the summer of 1987. That was a very long time ago. Whilst my mind was still working its way through this conundrum, the assistant then proceeded to say,

"You used to be my form teacher."

These words spilt out of her mouth. I was frozen in the moment. She was in my form class from my NQT (Newly Qualified Teacher) days; the first year, if not the first day of my teaching career.

I looked down and saw her badge: the name Rachel was displayed on it. I immediately knew who she was whilst simultaneously removing my face mask.

I was grinning from ear to ear. We both were. One crucial point would clarify that she was the woman that I was thinking of.

"When's your birthday?"

She began,

"I'm going to be..."

I stopped her mid-sentence and finished it for her.

"You're going to be fifty on the 5th of November".

Her eyes widened, her mouth dropped open, and she took a step backwards.

"Do you still go to that Pentecostal church in town?"

She almost fell to the floor.

"Oh my God, your memory is amazing! How did you remember all of that?"

I wasn't going to reveal that trick quite so quickly but remarked on how she still looked the same. Her hair was now straight and blond, a drastic change from the mousy brown wavy shoulder-length style of her formative years, but her eyes were unchanged.

"In fact," I said, "I've been decluttering and came across our old form picture this very week. What a coincidence. But how did you know it was me?"

She looked at me and a huge grin flashed across her face. "I do this every day. Customers are always giving me their details but when you said your name, I just knew it wer' you."

The questions flew out of our mouths, we barely answered one when another came. We were both giddy, excited, exhilarated, and full of all of those wonderful feelings when something amazingly unexpected happens. We constantly grinned at each other and couldn't believe what had just occurred.

Once we'd calmed down, we began to unpick the circumstances that led us to this moment. Rachel had been working at the store for years, and this was not her normal working day. Not only was she covering a shift for an absent colleague, but any of the staff could have come out to serve me. I then explained my wedding accessory story, that I rarely came into the store and if I hadn't noticed another customer paying with her card, I would never be here. What a serendipitous moment. She needed to see the class photograph and I promised to return with it the next time that I was passing by.

Curious members of her team appeared to identify the sources of laughter and having realised that normal service would not resume in the immediate future, they happily alleviated Rachel from her post. We were too engrossed in catching up on our past to notice the growing queue forming behind me. She was still in contact with a few of her former school peers and remarked that she would post it on social media, maybe we could get together for a little reunion.

We eventually exhausted our questions and said our goodbyes. I finally received my account pass, placed my mask over my mouth and nose, and descended the escalator. I was convinced that my mask did little to conceal the huge smile emanating from beneath it. This was truly one of my happiest days in recent times.

With my purchase in hand, I skipped home up the long hill and couldn't wait to deliver this amazing news to my family. I then completed the next logical step and sent a friend request to her on social media, knowing she would add me to the group with whom I had previously taught. I knew that something interesting was about to happen. Not necessarily in my favour, but as a teacher, being able to cope with criticism is an essential art. I was almost certain that some of my former form group would provide comments regarding their past relationships with me that were not necessarily favourable. Either way, this information would necessitate the inevitable regurgitation of old-school stories. With my friendship accepted, I impatiently waited to see how the messages would unfold. Any notification of my presence on their thread, could twist or prevent any possible emerging stories, so I decided to remain anonymous for the time being.

The first few comments were harmless and made me chuckle.

"I remember her getting married, but she didn't change her surname, she wer' just Ms instead of Miss Blake lol."

Then came the interesting one.

"When my dad was the caretaker, he said they found Mrs Michaels and the other PE teacher Mr Fallows in a cupboard naked."

Ooh, that rang a few bells. She was 50% correct, but I didn't want to reveal anything in a public forum.

My lack of patience got the better of me as I was intrigued to see how they would react once they knew that I was in the group. I announced my presence on the message thread.

"Hi, Ms Blake (doesn't feel right calling you Maxine). It's so good to hear from you."

This warmed my heart.

There are times when words cannot provide sufficient substance to say how I felt on that day. It had been thirty-four years since I had last talked to any of them. They were now approaching fifty-years-old and were all amazing women blazing their own individual paths. I was proud to have taken a small part in helping to shape their lives.

The news spread that I had made contact with a few of them, and arrangements were made to meet in the flesh. I was experiencing an interesting concoction of emotions. I was a little nervous, excited and apprehensive in equal measure. Whilst preparing for the evening, thoughts were constantly racing through my mind:

'What if we have nothing in common? What if they don't like me? What will happen if we don't get on?'

As usual my glass was half full, full of its usual doubts and fears.

We had all formed ideas in our minds on how we would all be in the future. I was the adult, and they were on the cusp of their teenage years. I just hoped that we all accepted the many changes that the years had forced upon us and reminisced about the good times that we had. The thought had also crossed my mind that they might even furnish me with additional stories to have enough material for my second book. It would also be interesting to hear the stories as experienced through their young eyes.

The evening came and went so quickly; I needn't have worried as it was so much better than I could ever have imagined. They reminisced on the type of teacher that I came across as. For once, I had to maintain some form of decorum and remained quiet, accepting their comments as gracefully as I could. I then revealed that I'd written a book that they might just be interested in a few of the characters, as they might be a little familiar. To further pique their interest, I reminded them of a few of the conversation topics that occurred in the staffroom at the time. Having heard this they were keen to furnish me with additional information on several of my old stories and continued with insights into a few new ones that had slipped my mind.

The following stories were developed as a result of our reunion.

YOU CAN'T UNSEE THIS

Jayne's Stories

We were lucky as our P.E. curriculum allowed us to participate in ice-skating sessions on a weekly basis for some of the year. It was always a pleasure listening to the latest tunes as we skated around the rink with our friends. We were constantly trying to look grown up and elegant whilst simultaneously trying not to look stupid in front of the boys. There was always someone that took our fancy.

One particular day whilst sitting in the school's minibus waiting for our Physical Education teacher Mrs Michaels, I turned towards the school building to note that she was running. This may not strike you as anything unusual, but she never ran anywhere no matter how late we were. Previously, I had only seen her walk swiftly, so this change of pace had gained my attention. She must have been in a rush as she diverted from her usual path that headed towards the gate. Instead, she took it upon herself to try and jump over the wall that surrounded the school. Mrs Michaels never ran anywhere, there is an obvious reason for this. She wasn't built for running or jumping fences as she was a little on the large size. Her pursuits quickly caught the eyes of everyone in the minibus. Conversations quickly halted as we all faced our new subject, mesmerised by the unfolding activities. It became apparent that she was ignorant of her new audience and was determined to overcome her new challenge. With both arms on the wall to steady herself, she leaned forward and tried to hoist her leg up onto it. This was swiftly aborted as her legs were too short to gain any kind of hold. She then decided on a different strategy; with her back against the wall, she bent her arms and placed them on the top, in an attempt to leverage herself up. She just couldn't get far enough off the floor, well, her legs dangled in the air for a short while. We all watched with our faces pressed against the windows as she fought against gravity and lost. After her third attempt, she eventually had to admit defeat. As she began to retrace her steps, she became aware that her attempts had not gone unnoticed. Her usually unobtrusive walk quickly became a walk of shame, her head and shoulders drooped as she approached us.

To say that she didn't look happy was an understatement. Maybe she knew how cruel children could be. To her surprise, and I'm sure total relief, a huge cheer erupted when she eventually boarded the bus. We never spoke of it again. Unsurprisingly from that day forward she reverted to her well-rehearsed walk to the gate.

***

This teacher's reputation preceded him. The whole student population knew of his existence whether they were taught by him or not. He had a particular sense of fashion and an interesting walk... well, more of a peculiar gait. His stroll was a constant talking point across the school. Wherever you were within the building, his familiar shape with bowed head, could be seen gliding along the corridors, with his feet refusing to allow any air between themselves and the floor, as he shuffled towards his next destination. He was already fully ensconced in the school history books when I arrived in the autumn of 1983. The subject of Computer Studies was still in its infancy; he was its solo expert and ruled the roost.

On this day, he had a new intake of pupils. There he was, with his purple rollmop jumper, a wardrobe staple. He was showing typical signs of male patterned baldness and maintained the look that had often been captured by many men who refused to acknowledge the marching of time. The sides and back were long to overcompensate for the dearth in the middle. The additional decoration to this look was the ever-present dusting of dandruff on his shoulders.

He addressed the class and said:

"You may call me Mr. Kendle, you can call me Killer Kendle but not under any condition will you call me Queer Kendle."

This held a different meaning in the 1980s.

What an introduction to your teacher. When she was a pupil, Jayne thought he was just a little peculiar.

Twenty-five years later, across the city, Jayne was waiting for her son outside the school grounds. She noted the outline and gait of someone walking within the grounds. There was a vague sense of recognition about it. She was immediately taken back to her own school days. She turned to her son and pointed out the man to him. She asked if he knew him. He quickly replied,

"Oh, that's Mr Kendle."

"Mr Kendle?"

"Yeah."

"Oh, he used to teach me."

She now had the opportunity to study him a little further. There he was, resplendent in his purple rollmop jumper, with the crown of his head showing signs of having received a little too much sun over the years, and the remnants of his hair resting on his shoulders.

As she recalled this story to me, I wondered if he had retained this jumper from all those years ago. The old adage of 'I have underwear older than you,' could be true in this case. I quickly made a mental note to declutter my wardrobe.

***

Shelly's Story

Sometimes things just don't feel quite right when out and about, and the only place to feel secure is at home. This was one of those times. Shelley was initially excited about her residential trip in the Peak District. White Rose cottage lay about ten miles outside of the Sheffield boundary, so it wasn't too far to be away from home for the first time. This morning she woke up feeling that things were not going to go as planned. Angela, the trip leader, wasn't a teacher, and things tended to go a little awry when she was in charge. The boys often tried to see how far they could push things before they were made to toe the line. To make matters worse, or better, it was also Shelly's birthday, she wasn't sure whether this was the company with whom she wished to be celebrating it with.

By the evening of the first day, she was getting upset, but she couldn't quite understand why. Was it her age? Her hormones? Both? She had no idea, but she was sure of one thing: she had had enough.

"I'm not liking it. I've seen the signs to Sheffield, I know the direction that I need to travel in, I'm goin' 'ome."

She was on foot and had failed to note the distance, the impending darkness and the fact that the staff would be worried. She grabbed her old friend Lisa for support. No request was made.

"Lisa, we're walking 'ome. This is boring, nowt's happening, and I don't like it."

She pointed to the sign in the distance. Lisa nodded in compliance. Without a word to anyone, they grabbed their bags and began walking in the general direction of Sheffield. They were happily meandering along a minor road, exhilarated as they had escaped the doldrums of the residential. Fifteen minutes into the walk, they became aware that there was a vehicle swiftly approaching them flashing its headlights. The darkness coupled with the approaching vehicle disarmed them as they now felt exposed by the roadside. The flashing lights increased in its intensity as the vehicle swiftly approached them. They froze, unsure of what their next moves should be. Their unease was further increased as the vehicle stopped behind them. The door slid open and ricocheted as it hit the lock. It rebounded and clicked as it shut. Shelly and Lisa remained rooted to the spot, facing forwards. It was then that the familiar dulcet tones of Angela's voice hit their eardrums,

"Oi... get in."

They didn't need to hear that instruction twice. They had been caught. With heads bowed and their tails beneath their legs, they swiftly made a hundred and eighty degrees turn in the direction from which they had attempted to escape. They mounted the minibus steps. Not a word was exchanged between the two girls. They were on the receiving end of a severe reprimand on their return journey.

***

Rachel's Story

At school, most teachers had a form group attached to them. These were identified by the teacher's initials, mine was 2MB. The register was taken, a brief tutorial given, followed by an assembly or the first lessons of the day. The format of the morning, provided the buffer between home and school life, thus allowing the pupils a settling in period.

Somehow, Rachel missed the opportunity to settle in with her peers; she was often late. She had another priority that needed her attention: her hair. This had become a common issue amongst many girls and a few of the boys. My memory of her is of a petite, very chatty confident young girl with sparkling eyes, a fringe and mousy-brown curly hair. I thought that it was naturally wavy, apparently not, she had to curl it every morning.

When challenged, her reply was,

"I wer' messin' with me 'air, coz I 'ave to curl it."

It became apparent that I did not appreciate her efforts. Rachel noted my reply,

"The next time that you're late for school because of your hair, I'm going to make you tie it back and we're going to straighten it."

She failed to acknowledge whether the threat worked. I can neither confirm nor deny that I had spoken to her in that way. The 1980s were certainly different times.

For my sins, I also taught her Physical Education. It was on her timetable anyway. In her annual report, I allegedly wrote:

"I look forward to the reasons why Rachel cannot do P.E. today."

I laughed at this quote as this sounded like something that would just fall out of my mouth.

Part 2: Let's Make it Short and Snappy

I'M NOT ALONE IN THIS

The following stories are being told from multiple perspectives.

I occasionally use this method to see if my students are paying attention. The answers are displayed on the board, in front of them, or often, both. Most of the time, I can almost see the synapses firing as they attempt the work. They still barely pass, some even fail. So much for reading through the questions before you start.

Similarly, when clear instructions are written on the board they ask,

"So, what am I supposed to do?"

Equally annoying is that look of confusion on their faces when you set a task, before you've even explained it, out comes the obvious statement,

"I don't know how to do it."

The list goes on.

***

For many years, my first school held a poor reputation in the city; the area was also the subject of discussion on the national news for all of the wrong reasons. Despite the daily battles with management on how to run the place, there were some good times. One day, I recall two members of staff walking down the corridor, both were women. One wore a very close-fitting jumpsuit with a slit to reveal her navel. (different times). They were deep in conversation exchanging pleasantries and smiling at each other. Two pupils were meandering down the corridor towards them. Without warning, Helen administered a severe tongue-lashing, leaving the pupils quivering in her wake. She resumed her conversation with Miranda where she had momentarily left it.

I love these strong women.

IS THIS ON THE SYLLABUS YET?

The Twelve-Step Programme of Zoom Survival:

1. How to handle parents from Hell.
2. If it doesn't work, just smack it, bang it or kick it: printer repair 101.
3. Ninja Moves: how to sneak away from the printer that you've just jammed.
4. Lies My Students Told Me: how to keep a straight face (so many lies).
5. The artist within them (a chapter of pictures of various genitalia drawn on school walls, desks and toilets.). Mmm, their own or someone else's?
6. Impractical Class Management in honour of the Covid year!
7. An outstanding teacher until the walk-through.
8. Be careful what you write in your emails.
9. Be careful who you write to, in your emails.
10. Yes. This is towards your exam mark and the other lies that we tell our students to coax them to complete their work.
11. How to cope with seeing naked parents in the background of a Google/Zoom/Teams meet.

12. What to say at parents' evening after you've seen naked parents in the background of a Google/Zoom/Teams meet.

ANSWERS ON A POSTCARD, PLEASE!

I was presenting a video about the solar system to a student who had a lisp and needed to work on his 'r' phonemes. He was constantly struggling and was often the butt of many jokes from his peers. When it came to the end of listing the planets, he said:

"Theyuz no appwopwiate way to say 'Uwanus'."

I looked at him and nothing came to mind.

I could summon no appropriate response.

Well, there isn't, is there? How to answer that question?

Answers on a postcard, please.

WHEN PARENTAL SUPPORT IS JUST A LITTLE TOO MUCH

A parent wrote a handwritten letter to my school asking the following questions:

"Can teachers slow down a bit? It is hard for us parents to do tons of homework. Please consider that we are just getting the hang of using all of these online resources, plus there's the fact that we are also working. We don't think our children are learning very effectively this way. We'd also appreciate it if you assign homework only on weekends."

On receiving it a few questions ran through our minds:

Was he the voice of all the other parents? Or just the parents of this pupil?

Has this student ever completed his homework?

He thinks that this is ok, doesn't he?

Is this a confession?

Where do we go from here?

The only reply was:

"Dear parent, we appreciate your concerns, but the homework is for your child to complete."

***

I was conferring with a student in class when his mum suddenly logged on to the same essay and began editing and rewriting it for him.

The mum was speechless when we told her we could tell when, and for how long 'her child' was logged on and working, and we could see what revisions were made.

The parent was a fellow teacher at our school.

***

I was reminding my students of a recent rule as reinforced by the vice principal at a meeting. The rule was that pupils must not bring balls from home to play with at break times.

So, at the end of the day, I said,

"Remember, your balls need to stay home from now on!"

One of my shy, quiet, studious kids decided to take advantage of the end-of-day chaos and grinned at me and said,

"You mean 'these' balls have to stay home?"

Whilst pointing to his nether regions.

***

World War One was the topic for this term. I thought I'd try something a little different and add an additional level of interest with the use of a fog machine to simulate a gas attack. I had hoped to engage the students with a sense of realism. I failed to realise that a fog machine would set off the fire alarm. After this occurred, we proceeded to find our places outside to await the arrival of the firefighters. Upon their arrival, they exchanged information with the school duty team and set off to identify the source of the emergency. We were eventually allowed back into the building and to our classrooms. Much to my surprise, our local fire chief was already situated in my room. His presence alone reinforced the fact that it was my error that alerted the emergency services. The children were obviously delighted, they presumed that I had pulled out all of the stops in an effort to make their lesson as realistic as possible. Fortunately, the fire chief was a keen history aficionado. When I explained the type of atmosphere that I was trying to create, he decided to give a little WWI talk to my class, therefore earning some much-appreciated kudos. From that day forward, each time a fire alarm went off other staff joked,

"Is Sir doing another World War One simulation?"

***

The school governors sent out an email to all of the heads of the trust for Literacy Month. The Headteachers of each school dutifully forwarded the email to their respective staff. This email had been circulated to hundreds of staff in the trust and yet somehow no one had spotted the typo.

The letter C had been added to the front of the title that read 'Literacy Month.'

The questions that sprung to mind were?

Could that have been auto corrected?

Who identified the grammatical error?

At what point did this occur?

Who did they tell? How was it raised in conversation?

So many questions.

TEACHER BLOOPERS AND POTTY MOUTH STORIES

There's an old Jamaican saying: 'Mouth open, story jump out.' To translate, sometimes we just lose control of the utterances that exit our mouths. No matter how much we try to catch and swallow them before they offend or surprise anyone, our words can tumble out, slapping the ears of all who happen to be in the vicinity.

We aim to be positive role models whilst being reflective and responsible. We do try to present our best selves as much as possible, but sometimes we fall just a little short of our targets.

These little quips are not what the teachers, including myself, had formed in their minds to say to their students. But once said, they cannot be unheard.

Enjoy.

***

"Look at the picture of my beaver."

***

"What are you doing? You're all jacking off!"

The room became silent.

She mentally processed her statement.

Shit, that came out wrong then.

She made a second attempt.

"Sorry, I'll try this again. You're all jacking around. My mind is still in the sewer this morning."

She laughed, and they eventually joined in.

She thought,

'They're twelve years old, they know exactly what I'm talking about.'

***

A beloved member of staff had unfortunately passed on and had left a lasting impression on our institution. On such a sad occasion, the staff decided to organise a tree-planting memorial ceremony at the school.

To ensure that the procedure ran smoothly, the Head had written a carefully phrased email to the staff.

"Dear staff, as you know the memorial service is to be held tomorrow to commemorate the life of our dear colleague. We have several of her close colleagues who have requested to say a few kind words. As we will be outside for most of the ceremony and showers have been predicted, please don't forget your willies."

I'm assured that our dearly departed staff member would have chuckled at his gaffe.

***

My zoom lesson was going well. As well as could be expected in these times. As usual, some pupils chose to have their cameras turned on, for others I just looked at a blank screen. Regarding distractions, the backgrounds added fuel to the fire. The pupils constantly asked irrelevant questions. Often, a parent would enter the room and start a conversation with their child, oblivious to the fact that everyone could see them. It was one of those days.

One of my kids was distracted by his dad.

He had just walked past the camera in his underwear.

"Daaaaaad.... I'm in a meet."

Dad replies, "WTF... Jeez, Mary Joseph and Moses, why didn't you tell me?"

I'm lost for words.

"Um,"

was all that I could muster.

How will I ever move on past this vision?

Parents' evening was going to be interesting then.

***

"Dude! Do you not see your beer gut covered in hair just hanging out for everyone to see?"

This dad had walked right up behind his son to see what was going on in his lesson.

The camera and mic are immediately muted.

I can only imagine the post-event father/son bonding moment.

Did he somehow think that he was invisible? Or that they had a one-way camera?

***

The principal walked into my class just as I was writing on the board. In her usual timely fashion, a student, shouted,

"Miss, you missed the letter L in the word public."

I might have thanked her but in the heat of the moment, I really can't quite recall what I said.

***

It can often be a no-win situation when I try to dissuade the students from drinking any of the fizzy drink ranges on offer. Planned lessons can be abandoned to discuss the merits of alternative drinks over their full-sugar counterparts. An examination of the nutritional content from the labels can often provide animated discussions. We had exhausted that subject when chewing gum was brought into the discourse.

I distinctly remember trying to say sugar-free gum. I immediately lost the argument when out came the phrase:

"Sugar-free cum."

All credibility was lost in an instant. Much respect was gained from my potty mouth though.

***

A student whose first language was not English once asked,

"What do you eat for breastfuck?"

"Pardon?"

I was sure I'd misheard.

 "Could you repeat that, please?"

"Breastfuck."

"Oh, oh oh, OK. Breakfast."

I quickly transformed this into a lesson on spelling and syntax.

My mind repeated,

'Please, please never say that again.'

***

The usual pre-lesson chat with my teaching assistant one day did not proceed as planned. I was discussing the idea of a counting activity. I accidentally called it a c*nt activity. He didn't have the heart to correct me, so I continued as if nothing untoward had occurred.

Somehow it has never been mentioned in our further discussions.

***

"I saw this great tutorial about making speakers out of cups. You take two Dix…"

I paused, tried to self-correct but it wasn't working. Heads shot up from their desks, eyes widened in anticipation to see how I would work my magic on this. I couldn't. I wanted to crawl under my desk and wait for the lesson to be over.

***

It was the penultimate day before the Christmas break. I had succumbed to the constant demands to watch a film. As I'm breaking one rule, I may as well break another, so I brought in a few snacks too.

The students were engrossed in the film, a perfect time for popcorn.

"Does anyone want any cockporn?"

Luckily, they were too engrossed in their film for this to even register.

***

Practical sports lessons often require swift thought processes and actions. One day, instructions were not as clear as they should have been.

"Can you go to the male teacher's office and grab his balls?"

We were due to practice basketball that day. My normally compliant student strangely refused my request.

An expanded description quickly followed.

***

"Now, just let me ejaculate something here."

Although the sentence was grammatically correct, it was slightly out of context. Being typical students, we immediately lost control. This teacher was still lost in his thoughts and was rather perplexed; he hadn't noted any particular line of humour in his dialogue or so he thought. A brave student asked him,

"How does one ejaculate something?"

He accepted his blunder rather gracefully.

***

As a music teacher, I've heard too many bum notes during all the stages of practical development, I'm usually quite patient when suggesting changes. A few times though, despite my attempts at gentle encouragement, when listening to a solo flute player struggling with one note in particular, I eventually said,

"Get the F out."

This could have been taken in many ways. Luckily, he realised that the subject matter was all about his musical abilities.

***

It was my first year of teaching, so I hadn't yet developed the teacher bag of tricks and quips that comes with the seasoned, confident educator. One of my pupils was Eric Cartman in live-action nursery form. I'm not a huge 'South Park' fan but as soon as this pupil's antics were discussed, the Cartman-esque jokes immediately flew around the staff room, so I quickly became acquainted with this style of humour.

One of his many memorable moments was when he told me he had a rock in his butt; he wanted me to assist him in getting it out. He kindly obliged by turning his bottom to me. I was of course horrified. My mind had instantly wandered down some very dark places. One specific thought was whether he had secretly caught his parents in flagrante delicto and as children often do, he was attempting to mimic the act. To my relief, it turned out it was just a cool rock from the playground in his bottom pocket.

I thought I had the measure of him when he caught me completely by surprise on another occasion. He needed help to correct his writing. I gently told him what he needed to do. He replied,

"Come on, you mean I need to redo the whole fucking thing?"

***

We used to start the week by giving the kids the opportunity to share their news from the weekend. I had a little six-year-old who stood up and proudly announced,

"I woke up this morning and there was a new dad in my mum's bed."

All of the kids sweetly clapped.

Oh, the joys of innocence.

***

It was our annual parents' evening for our year 9 students (10–11-year-olds). If the pupil attends with their parents/carer, I always like to open the dialogue by focusing on them with a discussion on their career goals. On being presented with this question, my usually quiet unassuming pupil responded by saying,

"Sperm Donor."

The silent stares across the table spoke volumes.

***

Years ago, I was the advisor of an after-school cooking club. One week we made pizzelles, traditional Italian waffle cookies. I explained to the class that the traditional flavouring is anise (aniseed), but I was using vanilla because it was my family's preferred option. One child announced to the group in a very excited manner, that his mum always uses anus in her pizzelles.

I'm usually open to unusual flavours but I'll pass on this one.

***

Our Enrichment Week is an opportunity for students to be engaged in extracurricular activities. For one of the sessions, a police officer visited and was giving a presentation on the subject of saying no to drugs and alcohol. As the topic was around not drinking and driving, one little boy said,

"My daddy don't drink and drive, he waits till the light turns red."

Luckily the officer didn't bother to follow this up.

***

Much to my surprise, a bouquet of roses had been delivered to my classroom. Having accepted them at the door from the school secretary, my assistant inspected the card attached to the flowers. She turned to me and gave me a pleasing smile, indicating that they were for me. My partner had finally taken the hint and was being just a little more public about our relationship, or so I thought. I have to admit that I felt a little smug. I wanted to continue teaching until the end of the lesson and dismiss the class before I read his message in solitude. My teaching assistant though had other ideas and insisted that I take a closer inspection of the roses, immediately.

This beautiful red bouquet with a white floral arrangement turned out to be quite a surprise.

They were not roses.

They were thongs disguised as roses. The white floral arrangement cleverly disguised small white cube shapes stuffed with money. A little bewildered by this, I thought that my partner had misread my hints. I then proceeded to read the card. They were not from my partner either but the father of one of my pupils.

The response that he received was not the one that he expected. At the end of the school day, I called his wife and asked her to retrieve the bouquet. Her reply was not for the faint-hearted.

I never saw dad again.

***

"All the monsters are horny."

As informed by one of my twelve-year-olds when attempting to use a dichotomous key to classify the monsters from the children's book 'Where the Wild Things Are.'

***

This year's topic for World History, was the Fall of Rome.

"And how do we know that Nero was crazy?"

A student replied:

"He stood on a hill above Rome and watched it burn while playing with his thingy."

He wasn't wrong, he just lacked the eloquence of expression.

The video we had just watched included a voice over explaining that Nero set Rome ablaze and stood high above watching it burn, playing the lyre and reciting poetry.

I had to face away from the class to recompose myself. As soon as I could, I stated,

"He played his lyre while watching a fire that he started."

We all know the story, but I think I prefer this version.

***

My usually quiet attentive nursery pupil did not appear to be his normal self today. He was continuously fidgeting and couldn't focus for even the smallest amount of time on the tiniest of tasks. He was constantly asked by the classroom assistants if there was anything wrong, but he refused to answer. As we approached lunchtime, I became more concerned as his level of distress continued to rise. I thought that maybe he had had an accident in the toileting department and was too embarrassed to tell us about it. Once everyone had left, we finally managed to have a chat. He eventually looked up at me whilst simultaneously pointing to his upper leg, stating that something felt funny on his thigh on the inside of his trousers. He couldn't expand on how he felt any further. I felt a little uneasy exploring that area unless it was out of necessity. I detected no obvious odour, so presumed that a toileting accident was not the case.

Having thought through my options, I asked him to reach inside to see what we could find. I was secretly hoping that it was just that his trouser lining had been misaligned against his clothing. With no further encouragement needed, he placed his hand inside his trousers and pulled out a pair of his mum's bright red thongs! We were both surprised at the find. He looked a little perplexed as to the nature of the item of clothing, so I hurriedly rescued the situation and told him that I'd look after them until his mum came to collect him later. The relief on his little face was immediately evident.

At the end of the school day, his mum arrived. I had to explain the situation and handed her the offending article. The heat emanating from her body caught me by surprise as did the speed at which her face changed from alabaster to a deep shade of beetroot. She avoided eye contact and quietly stated that she will never wash their clothes together again.

***

Ben, one of the nursery children, decided to be all grown up and attempt to pack his own lunch. During one lunchtime, as the children were unveiling their delights, a member of staff looked up as they were proudly displaying their provisions, whilst simultaneously casting an eye at their friends' meals and envying some of their snacks. His eyes were drawn to the familiar-looking can that Ben had proceeded to set on the table. Upon closer inspection, he noticed the beer brand proudly being displayed. He calmly approached Ben and asked a few poignant questions. The child proudly stated that he had packed his own lunch and thought that he'd try the can of soda that he'd seen in the fridge.

***

"I need some hand cream."

One of the children replied,

"I have some of my mum's that you can use."

He eagerly pulled out a tube of Vagisil.

***

A vibrator was once confiscated from an eleven-year-old. He claimed that he had no idea what it was, when he removed it from his sister's room.

***

A colleague suffered from frequent migraines and her students were aware of this. Thinking that she might be of some help, one of his pupils brought in something that her mum uses for her migraines.

A personal massager.

***

One little girl in my class was quite envious of the fact that her elder brother played football. I suspect that she might have been more jealous of the kit that he wore rather than the game that he played. One day she came into nursery beaming and wanted to show me her new shin pads. I loved her enthusiasm and bent down to admire her new form of protection. She eagerly peeled down her long socks to reveal a pair of sanitary towels stuck to her shins.

***

One of my students brought his mum's drugs into school. They were not the prescription kind. She came to the school frantically asking to see her son but would not explain her reasons. Unfortunately for her, the police were already there, waiting.

***

A sweet little girl brought a very special wand into school. It vibrated when turned on and even provided three levels of buzzing. The girl's family had recently settled in the country and had very little of their own belongings with them, so a lovely anonymous person gifted them a donation box... the wand had been included. The parents greatly appreciated the donation, to help their daughter settle more easily into the country, they gave the 'toy' to her.

On this day, the class was studying music, specifically different types of sound. Mrs Jarvis had apparently never seen this type of wand before. She was grateful for the child's thoughtfulness and placed it on a music stand. It made different sounds depending upon the buttons that were pressed.

The wand was returned to her at break time to play with. As she waved it around, Mrs. Clarke, the duty teacher noticed it and nearly died of laughter when she saw the girl casting spells. Nothing was mentioned to the pupil, but Mrs. Clarke rushed inside to converse with her teacher. Imagine her shock as the true nature of the wand was revealed to her. The children returned after their break to find that their musical appreciation lesson had abruptly ended, they were now studying local history.

At the end of the school day, songs are played over the intercom to keep the pupils in a positive mood as they caught their buses.

The song for the day was The Beach Boys 'Good Vibrations.'

SHOW AND TELL (NOT AS WE KNOW IT)

The following items have been brought into classes as points for discussion by pupils.

Enjoy...

***

A condom...

...the glow-in-the-dark type. Thankfully, as yet unused. The child thought it was a balloon.

***

Her mother's bullet vibrator...

She proclaimed,

"Watch this toy dance!"

***

An anatomically correct ice cube mould.

A pair of very embarrassed parents.

***

Baby blue furry handcuffs...

Coupled with the response to the offer of keeping them in a safe place until the end of the day:

"You can't take these, they're my uncle's!"

***

Her parent's adult videos for a movie party. My very quiet and reserved Teaching Assistant took it out of her bag and yelled,

"Oh, my!"

Try being the teacher that had to call her parents.

***

A Playboy Magazine...

The vice principal left a phone message for the parent.

"I have your *Playboy*. You may come to my office to pick it up."

He never did.

***

Her mother's diaphragm...

"It's Barbie's trampoline."

***

Her mother's birth control pills. She then proceeded to tell the class that these pills are the reasons why she doesn't have a little sister or brother.

***

A used condom from her grandmother's bathroom floor.

***

"I found this balloon in my dad's dresser."

***

A funeral flower spray that said Great Aunt. My student walked by the funeral home and saw it in the bin. She was so proud of the gift she had for me!

***

One of my nursery children brought in a picture he had drawn. It just looked like a scribble on a page. He said,

"This is a picture of the Ebola virus. If you get the Ebola virus you bleed from your ears and your eyes and then you die."

I can still see the traumatised faces of the class after they heard this. Later, when his mum picked him up, she said,

"Did he share his picture? I'm so sorry... We tried to get him to bring a toy, but he insisted."

***

A maxi pad...

Worn on his face like a moustache.

***

A tampon, swung by the string...

"It's a spider killer".

***

A shoebox full of empty plastic tampon applicators…

He said that they were rocket ships.

***

It wasn't exactly what she brought but what another student thought it was… The theme was 'Letter of the Week' and a child brought what she said was celery salt in a bag. One kid said,

"I know what that is! My mum smokes it."

When I called mum to talk about it, she blamed dad.

***

A red thong.

The theme?

Bring in something red for show and tell.

***

His grandmother's red sequined thong.

***

Her stepdad.

He was in an urn because the other kids didn't believe her when she said her stepdad was sitting on her mantle shelf.

***

Grandparent's day: Grandad's ashes.

***

A hip joint from his grandma's hip replacement...

I stupidly asked how they got it, and he said it was left over from her cremation.

***

A shoebox full of ashes from her deceased aunt, including little toys...

She was using it as a mini sandbox.

***

Grandfather's teeth and the following week, her horse's teeth.

***

A box of nail clippings.

***

A toenail, her mom's whole toenail ... stuffed inside her doll.

***

WWII grenades. No consultation was made with the teacher or his parents. This resulted in a full-on school evacuation and the bomb squad being called in. Luckily, they were inactive.

***

A picture of their cat with a big bag of pot.

***

A Marijuana leaf in the outstretched arms of a nursery child.

"I brought you a mint leaf."

Or so she thought.

***

Several specimen tubes of urine, clearly taken from a doctor's office, with labels and prepped for the lab. They were not his samples.

***

A snake and a live mouse for his snake to catch and eat whilst the class watched.

***

A full bag of ear wax.

***

Her great-grandmother's long hair.

***

The head of a cat that her dogs had brought into the
yard that morning.

***

A dog that smelled like a skunk! The owners were used
to the smell.

***

His dad's wallet.

***

Mum's credit cards... Dad said mum couldn't have them
anymore.

***

Head lice on a piece of paper.

***

X-rays that were stolen from a solicitor's office.

***

A dead greyhound.

***

Bull's eyes from the slaughterhouse.

***

A prosthetic leg.

***

Horse testicles in a specimen jar.

***

A bedazzled bong.

***

Her glass eye!

***

A scab collection.

***

His seven toes on one foot.

***

A dead robin from her freezer.

***

Parents' divorce papers.

***

A bean sprout about five inches long. He had put it in his nose where it had sprouted. It had to be removed at the accident and emergency room.

***

A hibernating wasps' nest.

IT'S ALL S**TS AND GIGGLES

Chris asked if he could use the toilet during our usual reading group time. Hand hygiene is vital, but we had learned that the multiple hand-washing signs around the building could be a little like wallpaper; they merged unnoticed into the background. The pupils constantly had to be reminded of this task on their return. I looked at Chris, and with the usual dip of my head, I was about to regurgitate my frequently stated phrase, when he interrupted me and exclaimed,

"Don't worry, I washed my balls... err, I mean my hands."

I froze. My mouth remained open, yet no words were formed. He looked startled, not knowing what to say or do.

On a need-to-know basis, I just didn't need to know.

The only thing to do was to snigger. He joined in too. The class looked towards us, intrigued as to what was going on. As is often said: this one's not for sharing.

***

My nursery pupil once brought me a turd on a crayon. No questions were asked as to who, how, why, where or when.

It wasn't really what I had in mind when I introduced them to the new concept of show and tell.

***

It was a typical Monday morning, and I was keen to find out what the pupils had been doing over the weekend.

"So, did anyone do anything exciting at the weekend?"

The responses were usually two-fold. They either jump out of their chairs, screaming to gain my attention, or almost dislocate their shoulder joints as arms fling themselves into the air whilst bottom cheeks clench to maintain contact with their chairs.

I noticed one little girl tilting her head and looking up at me. I was all ears.

"So, what did you do at the weekend?"

Maria went on to say,

"I went out to eat with my mum, dad, big brother and granny."

"Aah, a family day out. What kind of food did you have?"

"Pizza."

"What kind of pizza? Was it a pizzeria pizza?"

I'm not sure what I meant by that.

"Yeah. It was a diarrhoea pizza."

Mmm, I decided not to ask her how it tasted.

***

Our annual Field Day was fast approaching. A colleague and friend of mine had shirts printed up. It served several purposes:

- Maintained the excitement in the school.
- Helped to recruit more volunteers.
- Galvanised the parents.

A shirt was provided for every child in the nursery school.

Just in case anyone dared to forget, she created and sent reminder fliers to their homes. Every pupil received one.

It should have said,

'Don't Forget Your Shirt!'

She omitted a crucial letter.

The letter r.

This faux pas remained hidden from her until the following morning. The parents dropped their children off at the school gates unusually early, and then began huddling in groups waving the posters in the air and giggling.

In her usual animated manner, she strutted over to greet them. Her curiosity was piqued as she noted a few unusual behaviours. They were huddled together with the fliers in their hands. One or two were even waving them around in the air. They also appeared to be intermittently examining them whilst casting curious glances in her direction.

A few of the parents had started to exhibit an unexpected level of over-exuberance as they turned to face her. Smiles were plastered across their faces with the posters all facing outwards, in her general direction. Her strutting immediately halted, and a small gasp involuntarily emitted from her mouth. Her typo stood out unapologetically. Apart from wanting the earth to swallow her up, she had to do something, fast.

With her composure now firmly regained, she appeared nonplussed as she bravely announced that it was just her unique way of getting the non-compliant parents together and breaking the ice.

That's thinking on your feet for you.

***

It was the day of my final teaching observation by my University Lecturer. Despite the levels of stress these bring, they had been pretty error-free so far. Maybe on this day, I was just a little too relaxed and had my mind on other things. The lesson was ending and I held up the maths page that the pupils were to take home.

"Okay, this is your maths workshit for tonight."

There was a distinct hush.

In front of my lecturer, my evaluating teacher and the whole class, that word came tumbling out.

***

I was being observed by a member of the Senior Team and instructed my students to:

"Get your boobs out."

I don't even know what I meant by that sentence.

***

What's a shit shit?

It was my mouth's version of a 'cheat sheet.' That's how I felt about the homework that day.

***

One year, I had a group of six boys for two hours in a row every day. A couple of them asked to go to the bathroom every day, at the same time, like clockwork. One day I mentioned that they needed to use their break time to use the toilets. One boy's face lit up with a cheesy grin. He looked me dead in the eyes and said,

"A man can't poo in four minutes."

No response was forthcoming.

***

It was the morning break, John was due to move into his classroom to prepare for his next lesson. As he approached the room, an offensive odour hit his nostrils causing him to stop in his tracks. The stench was so strong that he had consciously changed his breathing pattern to prevent himself from heaving. He decided that this method wasn't working and swiftly marched in the opposite direction. The foul smell needed to be reported immediately, and he needed another room for his class, preferably at the opposite end of the premises. As his breathing quickened, he realised that the odour was engulfing him; he was suffocating and on the edge of a panic attack.

The nature and evidence of the malodour then unexpectedly presented itself. With their heads bowed low, a teacher and her pupils swiftly exited from a class directly to his left. Their stifled moans and cries rapidly rose in volume as projectile vomit splattered the floor, the walls and anything in its path. The nauseating smell had now been identified as human excrement and urine became freshly wrapped with a heavy vomit topping.

John found himself fully engulfed in this freshly mixed cocktail. As his mind struggled to make sense of the ever-changing situation, he noted that the teacher and her class were not only coated in a brown liquid substance, but it was also dripping from the walls and ceiling, leaving a sludge in their wake as they withdrew from the class.

The horror of the spectacle had now been displayed in its full glory. These poor things had been coated in shit. There was no pleasant way to describe their predicament. Having surveyed the scene, John peeled himself off the nearest wall that he had flattened himself against and loosened his tightened mouth as his jaws were beginning to ache. Immediate containment was necessary. His conflicting feelings of repulsion and anguish had to be put to one side as he needed to direct the traffic and minimise the effluence. The class was steadily guided towards the changing rooms where they were able to shower and change into any spare P.E. kit. Their clothes were bagged for disposal. Parents were called and provided with what must have been an interesting explanation. They were eventually collected and taken home with suggestions for them to seek advice on any medical interventions that would be needed.

The school was closed due to the high level of toxins in the atmosphere. The cause of the incident needed to be identified and actioned promptly.

The source of the offence was found to be the male toilets situated directly above the classroom. The old pipes were in need of a complete overhaul and had finally exploded, making its exit through the ceiling. The weight of its content in conjunction with the help of gravity only aided the speed of its downward momentum. Unfortunately, the poor teacher and her students were its unexpected recipients.

TEACHERS' CONFESSIONS (WE DO IT TOO)

The best place to let one rip is the cafeteria or gym.

In my second year of teaching, I was passing out papers and developed a case of walking farts and couldn't stop it… it was silent, thank heavens. I'll never forget a girl's expression. Through a screwed face she exclaimed,

"Ewww what's that smell?"

Another student boldly asked,

"Who farted?"

What else could I do but exclaim,

"Yeah, you guys' stink," and sprayed some air freshener.

***

A student in my second year of teaching had digestive issues and could be a little gassy at times. She once farted during a lesson. The whole class heard it and sniggered. She felt awful. Luckily for her I have digestive issues too. I farted so loudly that the whole room went silent. I asked them,

"What? Everyone farts. Sometimes it just pops out. I apologise. Now let's move on."

We all laughed together. It was a risky move, but it made her feel better, so I'll take that as a win.

***

Room changes between lessons. There are so many kids around… no one is the wiser.

***

Whilst explaining the intricacies of molecular structures to her Advanced Level Biology class, Cara had a momentary lapse regarding her present situation.

She released a large rasping fart directly toward the class. There was a momentary pause as she thought through some of the questions or comments that might arise. She thought,

'*Carry on regardless,*'

and continued with her written explanations on the board.

When she finally turned to face her class, there was total silence.

222

"Any questions?"

No one dared to reply.

IT'S ALL ABOUT FARTS

My youngest student burped, and he told me,

"Teacher, my throat farted."

***

I had the misfortune of overhearing one of my thirteen-year-old's telling his friends that he had farted. No big deal, it's natural I thought. He then clutched his bottom whilst appearing to squeeze his cheeks together. To my dismay, he then went on to express rather loudly that it felt like his poo was almost out. It's just how most boys are; the fascination with their bodily functions can take up most of their conscious thoughts. I couldn't be a silent listener any longer and found myself with the rest of his peers urging him to go to the bathroom. Fast!

Did he? Oh no, he hung on for dear life. He tried to focus on his tasks but distracted everyone else with his squirming, moaning and shifting from cheek to cheek until the extent of the internal pressure had built to such an extent that he couldn't hold it in any longer. He then ran, well, swiftly waddled, to the bathroom.

He emerged triumphantly from the bathroom with photographic evidence for his friends.

The fight to maintain any kind of decorum was well and truly lost.

I do have to pause and ask a few poignant questions here though.

'Why would anyone do that?

Did he wash his hands?

Why wait? Everyone knew what he needed to do.

Why, in a time of obvious desperation, would you be hunting down your phone?

Was this a deliberate ploy to gain brownie points? Excuse the pun.

Why show the pictures to your friends?

Why take photos in the first place?'

BACKHANDED COMPLIMENTS

"Your face doesn't match your voice. You have a beautiful voice."

***

"I like how smushy your hugs are. Your belly is like a pillow."

***

"Miss, I love how your arm feels, it reminds me of my grandma!"

She was playing with my underarm fat!

***

A nursery school child whose mother is pregnant, approached me.

"Ms. Delgardo, are you pregnant?"

"Oh no, I just look like this."

Another nursery schoolboy:

"Yup, she's fat."

In my earshot too.

My young hero, another nursery schoolgirl came to my defence.

"That's not nice…. She's not fat, she's fluffy."

***

"I love fluffy (plump) teachers, you can tell they think about their students more than themselves."

***

"I like how you dress. Your outfits are always matching, even your shoes and mask! But you might want to rethink that shirt… your belly is too big."

***

"You look like you've had a million babies."

***

"You're not fat, you're just thick!"

***

"Mr. F, you run fast for a fat man."

***

"I think it's nice that you leave your white hair and not dye it like my mum, because it's wasting money."

***

"I love how Merina's hair is black at the top and then blonde at the bottom… I wonder how she gets it that way."

I found this written on a note on the floor… my highlights were overdue.

***

"I love your hair! It has those shiny things in it!"

My grey hairs.

***

"You are so nice, but I think my mum should do something about your roots."

As she handed me her business card for her hair salon.

***

"Do you colour your hair?"

"Yes," I replied.

"I think it may be running out."

***

"Mr. Osbourne, did you know you have a bald spot on the back of your head?"

***

"Your moustache isn't as big as my mum's!"

***

"I like your fur."

She was petting my arm hair.

***

"Oh wow, you're furry!"

I forgot to shave that day and was wearing a dress.

***

"I like those lines on your forehead."

***

"You have nice cracks on your face."

***

"I love you so much that when you die, I'm going to throw you a real nice wake."

***

"You're not old, you've just lived a really, really long time."

***

"How old are you? You look young, but I know you can't be."

***

"I would be sad if your head fell off and you died."

***

"You don't look like you're almost ready to die."

It was on the occasion of my 50th birthday.

***

"I love your jewellery. Can I have them when you die?"

***

"I love the smell of old grandmas."

It was said with the uttermost sincerity.

***

One of my students opened a door for me, I thanked him. He replied,

"I always open doors for old people who are going to die."

***

"You look old. As old as some of these old library books. But at least you don't look as old as Mrs. Rumple."

***

"I like you better with your mask on."

***

"I am really disappointed in your choice of trousers today; those aren't part of your normal cute fashion."

I never wore them again.

***

"Do you ever wear make-up and nice clothes and brush your hair? I think you would look nice if you did, and maybe not so tired."

***

When I wore a nice outfit and straightened my hair a student said,

"Wow. You look like you really tried today."

***

"Wow... You finally did a good job matching your clothes today."

***

"Miss, you shouldn't wear makeup anymore."

***

"I love your style. I mean, all the other teachers are so fancy with all their jewellery, nice clothes, shoes, hair and makeup, but you're just so... so... casual."

***

"I like you better with glasses... they cover up part of your face."

***

"I like your outfit today... I didn't like that one last week."

Last week she looked me up and down and said,

"What are you wearing?"

***

Two of my pre-teens looked at my outfit, and one told me,

"You look like you're going to a wedding... that you don't want to be at."

***

"I feel like you are the type of person who gets really dressed up and looks really pretty and goes to bars. And then when men come up to you and hit on you or ask you out you very aggressively turn them down."

Apparently, I dress well, whereas most people my age just give up.

***

"You look lovely today."

"Thank you." Whilst secretly thinking,

'How was I looking yesterday?'

***

"I love your sweater, where did you get it?"

"Thanks, I got it at Kohls."

"Ah yeah, I shop there sometimes too when I want cheap clothes."

***

"Where'd you get that dress? It's kind of tacky."

***

"Wow, you do have more than one pair of shoes?"

***

I had an eleven-year-old who put his head on mine, hugged me, and said that I was his favourite teacher. Sweet. The head lice I got from him, not so much.

***

An eight-year-old gave me a note in a cute little box that read:

"You are the best teacher ever, probably."

***

"You're my fifth favourite teacher."

"But you only have six ..."

"Well, you made the top five."

***

"Mommy and daddy were doing the horizontal tango and daddy got a bj!"

This would've been awkward enough, but she came out with it in the middle of a parent's evening.

***

"Me and mam came back from the caravan early because she walked into the bedroom and dad had her clothes on."

***

"Daddy was fixing Mummy's sore tummy on the kitchen table, and she was making a lot of noise."

***

"Dad is allergic to latex, that's why I have so many brothers and sisters."

***

When discussing family with a five-year-old, I asked what her mum's name was, and she replied, "Mummy."

I said,

"That's what you call her, what does daddy call her."

To which she replied:

"Slapper."

***

We were discussing noises that we hear in the morning. I was thinking along the lines of nature.

"I hear my mum tell me it's time to get up."

"'I hear the toast popping up and the kettle boiling."

"I hear my dad do a poo. It's the next room to mine and he never shuts the door. He does it every morning as I get up. It stinks."

***

"I like the way it feels."

As said by a young male student while staring me dead in the eyes, refusing to take his hand out of his pocket.

THERE IS SUCH A THING AS A STUPID QUESTION

One of my favourite questions I've had from a parent is one who asked if I could change their daughter's grade by 2% to enable them to qualify for a scholarship.

"It's only 2%, so it's not as if it makes a difference for anyone else."

***

A parent during a more recent parent's evening:

"How old are you? Are you even old enough to have a degree?"

***

"Oh, you have office hours. Can you help him next week since there's no classes during your holiday break? Your schedule is open, right?"

***

"Oh, my child doesn't poo at home, we only feed him chips and bread… Can you work out a plan so that he can poo at school? We can then use it at home. Also, don't use sweets as a reinforcement, we care about his weight. Thanks!"

***

At the end of the year, a parent requested to see me and asked,

"Why is my child failing?"

"I have never seen your child."

"Well, he has a job. Can he make up all of the year's work by Friday?"

***

I had a student who asked me what my 'real job' was, after I finished teaching at school for the day.

***

"You don't work in summer, why do they pay you?"

***

"My daughter never listens to me at home. Can you tell her to listen to me?"

***

"Why does my son need to know how to write an essay?"

***

"Do you smoke weed?"

***

"Did you have to go to college to be a gym teacher?"

IT'S JUST MY OPINION BUT...

"You look like one of those nice pretty girls that surprises everyone by robbing a bank."

***

When my class found out that I didn't have any kids.

"You're pretty enough to have a baby daddy."

***

"Some teachers are way too nice. You aren't one of them."

***

"You're the only teacher I don't want to throw a chair at."

***

"All year long, you've turned to write on the board and not one time have you had VPL."(Visible Panty Line)

***

When I was pregnant, I had a nursery student tell me,

243

"You will be a good mummy. You make sure your kids aren't assholes."

***

A five-year-old walked around me sniffing my perfume. He then looked up at me and proclaimed, "Gee, Miss Merillo. You stink real good."

***

"Are you single? All the divorced dads were checking you out at open day."

***

"You should get married. You're too pretty to stay a virgin."

***

I taught ten-year-olds, our break time was at the same time as the seven-year-olds. One of them told me she liked the purplish-pinkish eyeshadow under my eyes because it matched my shirt.

I wasn't wearing eyeshadow.

***

I caught a student who had forged his parent's signature. The student wrote me an apology.

I'm very sorry I underestimated your smartness.

***

"You are so mean... but I think that's how you show me that you care about me. At least that's what my mum says."

***

"Do you smoke pot?"

"Why are you asking me that?"

"Because you're always smiling."

***

"You look like you took a pill to make yourself look good today!"

***

"You're always so calm! You must do drugs."

***

"When you're not here, my days are like a toilet. Everything just goes down the drain."

***

"Your decorations in your classroom remind me of how I decorate my room. I can tell you are trying really hard, but it's just not quite working."

***

"I remember you, you used to be so pretty."

This was said after I ran into a young student I used to work with.

***

"I'm naming all my farts after you."

***

"Miss, you look constipated today."

***

"You look like a superhero today. The green one. The Hulk."

***

"You're the smartest blonde I've ever met."

***

"You seem like a nice guy despite what they say."

***

"You remind me of Melissa McCarthy. I feel like you would totally throat punch someone."

***

"You're a much better teacher now than when you started here!"

***

"Gosh, Mrs. B, even for a white lady, you're white."

***

"I don't hate you as much as my other teachers."

***

"Mr. Fitzgerald is not the instructor I think he should be, but I've learned to live with it."

***

"Some people say you're pretty."

***

"Are there cameras in here? Because you always teach like the other teachers do when the principal is in the room."

***

"I like the sparkly stuff on your eyes. it matches your veins!"

***

"You're the dirty sock to my shoe."

***

"You're just like Batman, you both have major trust issues."

***

"You're the eye of Sauron."

***

"You don't understand. This is supposed to be a slack class. You've turned it into a real class where we have to work and learn!"

***

"Omg, did you get Botox?! You look so good!"

THE COCA-COLA BOTTLE INCIDENT

My teacher's instinct has switched on and is now on full alert. I quickly scan the room for any unusual activity. There's something not quite right in my classroom. It's just not the right type of silence; akin to the wrong type of snow on the train line. There's an eerie feeling in the air that I can't quite put my finger on. Today was just one of those occasions.

My anatomy introduction had gone quite well, and the students were generally working on their tasks. They tended to struggle with new terminologies as they were often quite long, complicated and alien to their tongues.

I started weaving through the desks, offering prompts and questioning the student's understanding. As I made my way to the back of the class, I noticed an interesting drawing on the front of one of the student's desks. With my curiosity now peaked, I slowly approached him, not wanting to draw undue attention to either of us. I noted that he had used a black whiteboard marker. The outline of the drawing bared a distinct resemblance to a glass bottle with a long neck. Not too dissimilar to an old-fashioned Coca-Cola bottle. The top was missing, so in effect, as the drawing was on its side the contents appeared to have spilt out onto the desk. At the opened end there was an arrow pointing down the neck of the bottle. I continued with my approach still withholding any comment. He quickly glanced up and noted that I had seen the doodle.

"This is my shaft."

I ignored the bait and paused behind him to support another student. The best reaction was no reaction, or so I thought. I just needed to be in close enough proximity to cut him off at the quick should anything untoward occur. He decided he was not going to be ignored and began to repeat his initial statement. With each phrase the volume increased. He had now succeeded in disrupting the class as they had begun to shuffle around, eager to view 'his shaft.'

Plan B had to be invoked. I positioned myself in front of his desk.

"This is my shaft."

He eyeballed me, daring me to react. The class embarrassingly giggled. I blurted out,

"If this is your shaft, you really need to see a GP pretty quickly."

They loved the teacher put-down and were not shy when expressing their appreciation.

I thought to myself,

'Was that the best you had to offer?'

This could have gone oh-so-wrong, but it did the trick as he never disrupted my lesson in that manner again.

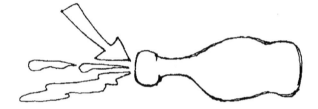

Part 3: Catching up with Old Friends

A SUBTLE INSTRUCTION BY THE ELDERS

Jay's Stories

I met Jay in my first teaching post. At the beginning of my career, I used to take public transport to work. This often entailed meeting the pupils much earlier than I would wish to at the beginning of my teaching day. Jay lived en route and thankfully provided me with a lift to work, saving me money, time and those early student encounters. I had forgotten about these little pleasures until reminded of him by another former colleague. The only thing that I could recall was that he wore driving gloves.

Here are his stories.

***

"Don't keep going over there, they've got a bigger budget than us. We're at war."

This was a young teacher's dilemma. Before you know it, you've been well and truly sucked in. It was a case of us or them.

When Jay first began his teacher training course in Sheffield, one of his placement schools was so large, that it felt like a small town. There were three staffrooms across its campus: one mixed and one each for the men and women. Within the men's staffroom was a dartboard and pool table, rather like an old-fashioned pub tap room. He had never ventured near the women's staffroom; it was out of bounds. Each Friday, as per the school tradition, the staff marched en masse to the pub (apart from those poor unfortunate souls who were scheduled to be on duty). The imbibing of alcohol was de rigueur for the time period. For Jay, the young teacher, returning to work to teach after a few pints, brought with it another level of danger. He taught design technology and, as such, was solely responsible for the pupils handling potentially dangerous equipment such as chisels, bandsaws and hammers. It was a miracle that no serious accidents occurred. On reflection, he can't believe that he allowed himself to get sucked into this culture. Health and safety procedures were not as it is today.

As with many schools, the pupil's home circumstances could be very challenging. The multiple levels of deprivation were a constant challenge, yet despite this, the children displayed unimaginable strengths to rise above it. They were often streetwise, mouthy, and oozed self-confidence within their own kingdoms. School trips were arranged to enlighten, engage and inspire them. As soon as they were out of their familiar surroundings, they became as timid as mice.

A trip to Barmouth in Wales was of particular significance. The students were camping in a farmer's field with Jay and three other established members of staff. In the middle of the first night, the pupils started to feel ill and began to vomit. Two members of staff were quick to follow in succession leaving the remaining unaffected. Unfortunately for Jay, the only other healthy member of staff could not or would not deal with vomit. Poor Jay had to be nursemaid and general slop bucket cleaner for the whole of the student and staff body. After a good clear-out, they rapidly recovered. The irritant was never discovered. On returning to school, he had gained a new title: 'The Vomit King.'

***

The summertime was a period in the UK that most students both anticipated and dreaded in equal measure. It signified the longer, warmer days and the eagerly awaited long holidays that preceded the start of the new academic year. Before this occurred, each student had to endure a summer of exams. The tradition was to sit them in either the gymnasium or the assembly hall. There may be as many as two hundred children sitting these exams simultaneously. They were scattered over the school with the majority in the larger spaces. The teaching staff would supervise. The usual format would be to position themselves at the front, back and sides of the space to ensure maximum coverage.

Jay was stationed at the front of the hall; the students were all sitting facing him. Mr Marples, an established member of staff, had positioned himself at the back, facing Jay. He was a large man, both in height and character and was carrying a little too much weight around his girth. He also sported a retro moustache; well, more dated than retro, it was quite full and drooping at the sides down towards his lips. Some might even regard it as 'a porn star moustache.' The supervisors positioned at the sides took it in turns to become the floater. They would wander up and down the aisles providing additional equipment, or should the need arise, they would escort the student to the toilets. After an allotted time, they would all rotate positions. As this was to be Jay's first time, Mr. Marples had thoroughly briefed him on the procedures, expressing the gravity of the position that had been bestowed upon him. He was to read out the rules and regulations, check that they were given the correct papers, reiterate the times that they were allowed to leave, and then finally start the clock in order for them to turn their papers over.

Having been given this prestigious position, Jay held it in the highest regard and as a relatively new teacher, he was keen to impress. Every process was to be executed efficiently. He had completed his instructions to the students and judiciously noted down the exam start time on the official sheet. Having settled into his position, he then looked up from his paperwork to note peculiar behaviours being displayed by Mr. Marples at the rear of the hall.

He was goose-stepping, jutting his neck out with arms splayed out at the back, similar to some aspects of the mating dance from the Birds of Paradise. He ended with a salute and a mock clicking of his heels. Every few minutes he'd turn to face the front to check Jay's reaction. With the students all facing towards Jay, none of them could detect the shenanigans taking place behind them. Jay had no choice but to observe this full transformation of a respected member of staff to a circus entertainer. He bit his lip in the hope that the pain would distract him. Mr. Marples regained his composure and sat down. Jay quietly breathed a sigh of relief, presuming that the display had come to an end. Five minutes later, he was up again, acting out a soliloquy of Monty Python's dead parrot sketch, bashing an imaginary parrot on his table whilst arguing with the equally invisible pet store owner. Minor guffaws exited from Jay's mouth, weakly disguised as coughs. These displays continued throughout the exam, with Jay forced to be the reluctant solo audience member.

The end of the exam also signalled the end of the comedy show. As they collected the papers, a wry smile crossed Mr. Marples lips.

No explanation was sought, and none was given.

SENIOR MANAGEMENT STORIES

It's Wednesday, and I'm on duty. For the staff who undertake this role, there are many responsibilities: during the break times, we need to be visible in key areas of the college. We are also the first port of call should there be an incident of any kind. If a skirmish occurs, we take the lead role in sorting the issues, minimising any audience viewing or participation. If I was lucky, I'd coast through the day with the minimum of interruptions: maybe the perfunctory student ticking off, a little chivvying along to their next class, or the odd luxury of chatting to them to catch up on their latest news. If I was unlucky, it would be a coded message on the walkie talkie, resulting in me leaping up the stairs to an all-out fight, a teacher in tears, or both. Today was a little different.

It was the afternoon break, and just one more session to go before the end of the day. I allowed myself the luxury of a small smile. We were speedily approaching the point where I could resume tackling some of the never-ending tasks amassing themselves in my inbox. The break time ended with little incident, students were still meandering around the plaza, so needed a little persuading to head to their last lessons of the day. With that task completed, I found myself alone with the vice principal (VP). I gingerly took the opportunity to take advantage of the situation. I needed to sound him out on a few ideas that had been mulling around in my mind for some time. Despite having an open-door policy, he was rarely available. It was now or never.

I carefully pored over the ideas in my head, sequencing my sentences together. I opened my mouth and exhaled just as our walkie talkies burst into life.

"Code 101, can the Duty Manager go to F02 please?"

We gave each other that familiar look. I began to pace towards the stairs.

He interjected.

"It's OK, I'll handle this."

Technically it was my call, but I was happy to relinquish my role as I relished the privilege of witnessing him in action. He climbed the stairs two steps at a time, and I followed in his wake. The room in question was immediately to the right of the stairs. We instantly knew what the issue was. The teacher stood outside of the door with the accused student who was familiar to both of us. When a student is known to most of the college staff, it's rarely because they were an upstanding member of the student community. We both faltered as the odour (or aroma, depending on your perspective) hit our noses. It wasn't an attack on our senses, more of a full-on Blitzkrieg. I was endlessly slapped in the face with the stench of cannabis. It was potent. The classroom door remained ajar, and we were acutely aware that the stench was rapidly wafting its way down the corridor. The thought had crossed my mind, with that level of intensity, the whole class could be stoned too. The teacher's mouth rapidly fired out information to explain the scenario; we raised our hands as a signal to slow down, we sensed both panic and anger in his voice.

"...no respect for authority... continues to blatantly break the rules... offensive... no desire to learn..."

We failed to halt his verbal bombardment, so allowed him a moment or two to unburden himself. He slowly, with each passing sentence, began to regain self-control.

We had a situation developing on our hands though, because of the drugs, the students couldn't remain in the classroom. We needed to act swiftly, and the teacher needed time to regain his composure. After a quick discussion with the VP, the class was sent to the café for a short break. This served a dual purpose: it gave us time to find an empty classroom and provided the teacher with an opportunity to calm down, sort himself out and move any equipment necessary. The accused student was then taken downstairs. He couldn't be searched against his will as this could be deemed as an assault, and he fastidiously denied any knowledge of drugs in his system or on his person. It would also have been difficult to prove given the classroom conditions. In full view of everyone in the café, the VP stood with his hands on his hips and thought about the next move. The student faced him with a slight smirk developing. He thought he'd won.

"Right then. See this line? Walk along it and turn around when I say so."

'Brilliant.'

He was being given a sobriety test. I immediately thought of many other humiliating tests that could have been performed in front of his peers. Those thoughts were quickly dismissed. They had front-row viewing, courtesy of the café windows, but they were trying not to be too obvious.

He happily obliged but couldn't decide which line he should walk along, so he tried them all. Unfortunately, the other lines were a figment of his imagination. He had reached the end of his imaginary lines, turned, and wryly beamed at us, revealing his teeth. Our blank faces hid the internal smiles. As much as he tried, this was one test that he was not going to pass. He had failed miserably. The battle was not yet over, and the odour was still lingering. The conversation resumed in the VP's office, where he guided him through the next stages of the disciplinary procedures. He had to remain seated on the bench in the plaza with all the doors open until a parent arrived to take him home and was ordered not to return until his formal hearing.

THAT EMBARRASSING TUG FROM BEHIND

The year was 2004, and the college was freshly built and occupied by its equally excited staff and students. We were the first purpose-built sixth-form college in our city and were proud to be setting the high standards that would help our young people to excel and forge their paths towards their glittering futures. Our young Principal Nigel was our guiding light and we stood proudly behind him, knowing that these opportunities were given to only a few to create something out of nothing. He had a vision and together we were to see it through.

Each day brought its own excitement. One day I noted Nigel standing outside his office at the top of the stairs. He was overlooking the plaza, the epicentre of student life during their downtime, and was perusing his new kingdom with a small grin on display across his face. It must have been so satisfying seeing your vision come to fruition. Our new students were beginning to mingle well. The staff were eagerly chatting with them, continuing to create the welcoming ambience that we were keen to portray. Classical music was being pumped through the main congregating areas, research had found that this helped to create a calming studious atmosphere, some of us were yet to be convinced of this and would watch and wait.

Break time was almost over. I stood in the middle of the plaza, calmly ushering the students to their next classes. My eye caught the movement of Nigel as he made his way down the stairs and across the main congregating area. This was not his usual walk; this one had just a little more purpose and direction, he was heading across the floor to the opposing set of stairs. I hadn't noted anything untoward happening so my gaze remained transfixed to see if anything was to become of this. Having previously seen him in action, I admired the calm demeanour within which he carried himself and how he was able to defuse situations without further escalations. Maybe there would be another lesson to be learned here, so I watched and waited. He swiftly made his way through the ambling students who were causing an obstruction on the stairs. The cadence of his movement changed. A student immediately began to ascend the stairs, rather too quickly I thought, swiftly followed by the principal. They veered right at the top of the stairs and were immediately out of view. I had failed to decipher whether there was a potential incident that he had tried to diffuse or whether this student was just in his path. I made a note to ask later as curiosity was getting the better of me.

I never managed to ask him about this, but I was reminded of the incident many years later at the retirement celebration of our latest principal. He happened to be standing in the plaza with his old friend and our first vice principal. Both were reminiscing on their early days and the many characters who had passed through our doors. Eighteen years later, I was to finally hear the story from the man himself. The story was much as I recalled, except I hadn't spotted what Nigel had called 'the exposure'. We didn't have a uniform policy as such, just that students should be respectfully covered and bear in mind the feelings of others when considering their mode of dress. This student appeared not to have received the memo.

Nigel recalled,

"I remember thinking, Oh no, that's much too much exposure for anyone. He needs some adjustment and a quiet word. I'll just help him to adjust his trousers as he's forgotten his belt. Once I'd made my way through the crowd, I saw the evidence glaring at me: there they were, two full moons rhythmically making their way up the stairs seemingly independent of their owner. So, I thought I'd help him out. I hooked my fingers into his belt loops to hoist his trousers up. He didn't take to this very well as he immediately bolted up the stairs two at a time. Unfortunately for me, I still had my fingers securely threaded through the loops and couldn't untangle myself. As you know, I'm no athlete."

I raised an eyebrow in agreement.

"I found myself running at full speed behind this student, desperate not to fall flat on my face, whilst simultaneously trying to maintain some sense of decorum and preserve the student's dignity. This was no mean feat. He didn't appreciate my efforts. It wasn't my most successful plan."

I was delighted to finally have a satisfying end to the story, but not the one I'd expected to hear.

YOU DON'T RECRUIT TROUBLE!

Unfortunately for the new Head of the Centre, who was a former principal of a small college, his strapline could no longer be adhered to.

He was no longer the king of his castle running an independent college, but one of many Heads of Centre, under a newly merged super college with satellite centres scattered across the city. Begrudgingly, he had to take orders from above and relay them to the staff. The original staff who knew better, still called him the principal.

As a general rule of thumb, Level One students across the UK have either had an incomplete education or held minimal qualifications and were at the lowest levels of attainment. Once they have entered post-sixteen education, the aim was to provide a generic course with a focus on an area of interest, if possible. The vocational opportunities available to them at this point though, were limited.

Dave taught one such course. The area of focus for these students was sports and he taught the computer studies element.

During the first few weeks of teaching, James, one of his students entered his room, he was closely followed by a familiar smell: Weed. Such was its proximity to him that he appeared to be wearing like a cloak. Unwilling to tackle the issue immediately as it would have meant further class disruption, Dave decided that he would hold a conversation with James at the end of the lesson. He was initially pleased with the way that he'd dealt with the subject matter; he felt that it was non-confrontational and most importantly that James had understood the underlying message. He began his approach:

"I don't know what you do at break time, but you need to stand further away from the other people smelling of weed. I can smell it on you but I'm sure that you don't smoke it. So this is just advice for the future."

He left it at that.

Later that afternoon, he received a call from his Line Manager requesting his presence in his office. Upon arrival, Dave was handed a phone with the explanation that there was a parent on the receiving end of it with whom he ought to talk to. Allegedly, he had accused his son of smoking dope and he stated that his son has never taken it. During the conversation, it transpired that James had gone home and talked to his mum about the earlier conversation. He might have missed a few important details but had ensured that he had declared his innocence to her. Having expressed the injustice of being unfairly blamed, he wanted his mum to defend him. He left any possible further actions to be taken in her capable hands. This had then been relayed to his father, who was now rather irate, to say the least.

Dave put the phone to his ear and had to endure a deluge of abuse from James' father. Rather than listen to this any further, once the father had inhaled for breath, Dave forcefully interjected to tell his side of the story.

He explained,

"Your son came into the class smelling of dope. I didn't bring this to his attention immediately but waited until the end of the lesson. I took him to one side and specifically didn't accuse him of smoking but that those surrounding him were. I told him he should stand further away."

This news upset the father further, who exclaimed,

"I'm going to take him out of the college and send him elsewhere because I don't want my son in a place like that where people smoke dope."

Dave chuckled,

"Where are you going to send him?"

"How do you mean?"

"Well, most places including the top public schools have this issue; so just tell me where you're going to send him?"

After a brief pause, Dave could hear the father having an incoherent debate with someone in the background; he thought that he recognised the voice as being that of James. An uncomfortable lull followed. Having returned to resume his discussion, James' dad appeared to have had a complete change of heart as the extent of the problem had been revealed to him. He pleadingly stated,

"Listen, I've never had anything to do with dope, I wouldn't even know what it smelt like. How do you know?"

This could have been tricky, but Dave was quick off the mark.

"Well, I've been a customs officer for ten years."

The father quickly concluded that his son should remain at his present establishment as it was as good, or was no worse, than the others. Dave withdrew from the office with a sense of accomplishment.

The following day, James was taking part in a staff versus student football match. He was marking a very well-known former professional football player who just happened to be playing for the staff team. He never managed to touch the ball but dined out on the story that he played against him for years to come.

He was as good as gold from that day forwards.

**

Dave's experience had taught him that whatever strategies he had used to enthuse his computing class, it was always a struggle to keep them focused. His class followed Mick's practical sports session. Being a former professional footballer and a new teacher, Mick had a few interesting techniques in his repertoire. Dave approached Mick and gave him some advice. This wasn't necessarily for Mick's benefit as a new teacher, but for Dave, to aid his classroom management.

"They'll have to be sitting down with me all lesson and they're not going to like it very much. Whatever you do, tire them out, start them running as soon as they're through the doors at 9am and don't let them finish until the lesson ends."

Mick was more than happy to comply with Dave's advice, even though his lesson was ninety minutes long. A weekly catch-up would take place during the break time between their lessons. Mick would report the class's progress to Dave. It would usually begin with something like this,

"Dave, you'll never guess what they've done now?"

There would be the inevitable roll of the eyes from Dave as he knew just how tricky they could sometimes be. On one such occasion, the shenanigans got a little out of hand.

"They've broken each other's arms!"

"What?"

"The ambulance has just left with the two of them in it."

Before Dave could pry him further for an explanation, Mick continued,

"They decided to have a little competition and see who was the strongest. They faced each other and interlocked their arms. With their clasped hands together, each would forcefully push the other along what they presumed would be their weakest points, their forearms. It was quite funny at first, but after a while, neither of them would give in and I could see the pain on their faces. They were constantly pushing and pulling and groaning in pain. It got to a point when the screams continued to increase. I took one look at their arms and noticed not only were their arms heavily discoloured but looked misshaped too. So, I decided that an ambulance would be needed for both of them. I don't know how I'm going to explain this to everyone?"

There was a long pause followed by a groan.

"What about the Accident Form?"

Dave could only reply:

"Good luck with that."

***

A 'get rich quick' scheme rumour had begun to circulate in the college. Its target range was young men aged eighteen plus. One student couldn't believe his luck and decided to take advantage of the offer before it ran out. He acted immediately, foregoing his next lesson. With the details of the city centre office memorised, he set off to earn his fortune. He duly arrived at what appeared to be a discreet part of town for these matters. He allowed himself a nod in anticipation.

He found the entrance, inhaled, opened the door, and stepped inside. He waited by the door and perused the room, noting that there was something slightly amiss. The age range of the candidates was not as he had expected. They were all quite old, probably over 65, and there were women present too. Were they there to support their partners? This was most strange. Having tentatively stepped further into the building, he then noted the banner across the far end of the room.

In bold yellow letters were the words, 'AGE CONCERN'.

In his urgency to 'get rich quick, he had not only chosen the wrong entrance, but he'd also failed to read the large sign attached to the top of it.

He stepped outside and looked to his left; there he saw the sign he was looking for: 'Sperm Donation Office.'

***

Friday evenings after work used to be the recreational time for staff. Football was their game of choice. Dave was not a player as such, more of a spectator. Alan though loved his football. They often had a few spectators from within the student cohort admiring their finesse and skills and the staff didn't mind showing them how the game should really be played. A few weeks into the regular friendly sessions, both members of staff noticed two young men hanging around, looking as though they were there for alternative means, possibly of the illegal kind. The occasional student would leave the sports hall with one of the boys and swiftly return. As the staff were occupied with their recreational pursuits, it was difficult to identify any actual illegal activity. Nevertheless, a close eye was maintained on the young men's activities and if any evidence was forthcoming, they would be quickly removed.

The following Friday, they presented themselves again, this time, one of them had the presence of mind to bring an enrolment form with him. When approached by Alan, he had the perfect ruse, he explained,

"I'm just filling this out."

It was 4pm and not wanting to miss the chance of recruiting a new student, Alan abandoned his beloved game and escorted the prospective student into his office. He thoroughly explained the rudiments of the enrolment form from the beginning to the end. This potential student had entered the premises at the end of the day, on the last day of the week, so, because of his dedication, he deserved his undivided attention. This whole process would take fifteen minutes on average to complete, maybe thirty minutes if you had to find evidence. There they were, two hours later at 6pm on a

Friday evening still in the office. Alan was being fastidious. For good measure he threw in a few tests for any additional help that this future student might require, dyslexia and dyscalculia questionnaires emerged and were completed, no stone lay unturned. Alan couldn't do enough for him.

His friend on the other hand, the one with the illegal substance in his bag, didn't know what to do with himself. In essence, he had no excuse for being in the building and there was nowhere to go or hide. To make matters worse, he was surrounded by teachers. Eventually, the staff ushered him out of the building as he couldn't possibly be left to his own devices unattended. Having expended all of his energy and time completing the forms, this brand-new student exited Alan's office; only to discover that his partner in crime was nowhere to be seen. His level of distress was all too visible. On realising this, Dave approached him and continued to rub salt further into his wounds by stretching the truth somewhat.

"Oh, your mate's gone. I saw him going for the bus."

The young man could hardly contain his anguish; not only had he spent his precious time enrolling on a course that he had no intention of attending, more importantly his supply of weed had disappeared with his accomplice.

Their regular Friday evening appearances ceased with immediate effect. Did the new student begin his studies?

Of course not.

***

The period approaching Christmas was always a little tricky; staff were exhausted, and the students' minds seemed to be engaged elsewhere, so the educators and those being educated were increasingly at loggerheads. Everyone was a little tetchy, the students couldn't see the point in being taught at the end of term, whilst syllabuses needed to be completed. Lunchtimes could be particularly contentious, so additional rules were put into place. The Pine Grove Country Club resided on the college's doorstep and was the favoured drinking establishment for both staff and students. As per the usual rules, the students could leave the premises at lunchtime but if they were to imbibe any alcohol, they could not return. This was of particular relevance as many of the students were apprentices working with machinery.

Dave's last class of the year happened to be from 7–9pm. Considering the relatively empty classrooms towards the end of the afternoon, he wasn't expecting anyone to attend but had prepared some work just in case. Three of the apprentices duly arrived. The conditions of their training required that any absences were to be reported to their sponsors. They were aware that their places were highly sought after, so they couldn't afford to put a foot wrong.

In his wisdom, Dave thought that it would be prudent to present them with something uncomplicated to view that could create a little discussion: a clip from 'Boys from the Black Stuff,' or a documentary of a similar ilk. At that time, if the class was in an outside hut away from the main building and a video was to be shown, the studio had to be booked within the main site. Having moved to the studio, they began to watch the documentary, only to be interrupted by a commotion outside. Dave disappeared in the direction of the noise and was faced with a view of three students vocally wrestling with Eric the principal. Each side was giving the other a verbal battering with no sign of anyone backing down. The students were drunk and could not be reasoned with. Equally, Eric was not putting up with this nonsense and eventually bellowed,

"You're banned from the college."

One of the boys fired back,

"You can't throw me out of this college, only the principal can do that."

At this stage it's poignant to highlight Eric's attire. Today, as with the other four days of the working week, there was very little to differentiate between his work and leisure wear. He was garbed in a sports jacket with patched elbows, a Viyella shirt and a yellow knitted tie. The response to say the least was unexpected. Eric, who was not a small man by any sense of the word, drew himself up to his full 6ft 3in height, leaned over the student and bellowed,

"I am the f*****g principal."

Realising his error and that there was no coming back from this, the student distanced himself, looked up to him and responded,

"Well, if you're the principal, I don't think much of your f******g tie."

Off he ran, as fast as his legs could carry him.

Eric was not finished; this incident had fired him up even more. Having spotted Dave retreating to the studio, he followed post-haste and entered the room, determined to deliver his message.

"What class are those lads in?"

Dave could only reply,

"Well, they're in mine, Eric."

"Who are they? I want them found and contacted now."

There was a small pause whilst Dave pondered the instruction.

"It's Christmas Eric, so I can't contact them now. Fortunately, I'm a good teacher and have a picture of them all."

He proceeded to open the register to reveal the photos. Without hesitation, Eric pointed,

"Him, him and him, bring them to me the first lesson back next year."

Dave tried to defend them by stating that they were engineering students, indicating that they were not studying full-time. Eric was not going to budge.

"Make sure it's done."

The three students who were still in the class silently witnessing the conversation, were sent home.

Ever the dutiful lecturer, Dave ensured that Eric's message would be immediately dispatched to the engineering member of staff. He was to be the first person to teach the students after the Christmas break. He explained the situation in an email and asked him to make an appointment with Eric for them on the first day of term. He ended by stating that he would leave it with him and pick it up in the new year.

The holidays came and swiftly disappeared; everyone had now returned for the new term. The engineering students completed their first session. As planned, the three named students were escorted for their allotted appointment with the principal. Eric was not one to forget any minor detail and the boys had no idea of what was in store for them. Suffice it to say, once you have received a severe reprimanding from him, it was not quickly forgotten. Apart from the fact that most of the college would be made aware of it, they could not afford to protest too strongly as their future careers were at stake.

Break time had ended. The students entered Dave's classroom, found their seats and sat down. He cast an eye over them to review the situation and assess any behaviour management techniques that he might need to utilise. The atmosphere was tense, maybe he needed to revert to the new teacher handbook: don't smile, no social interaction, get straight on with the lesson. He gave it some consideration but felt a little sorry for them. They were generally well-behaved boys who were caught by the wrong person whilst under the influence of a little too much Christmas spirit.

He was ruminating about the scenario for far too long and must have been staring at them, deep in thought. One of the three looked up at him, sniffed and said,

"And I don't think much of your f*****g tie either."

With that, the ice was broken.

***

One of Dave's main interests was Travel and Tourism. Each year, he helped to organise a trip, either within the UK or elsewhere in Europe. This year, he had arranged a trip to Paris. There were six or seven very responsible Travel and Tourism students who could afford the cost and time to attend such an event. To make this viable, they were to be journeying with twenty Art and Design students. They were given the usual pep talks regarding behaviours and responsibilities, but these seemed to have fallen on deaf ears. The first night out in Paris was horrendous. To say that they were behaving like British louts was an understatement. The imbibing of alcohol appeared to have been a recently introduced pursuit and they could maintain no sense of decorum in public. As it was the first night of the residential, Dave hoped that they were just stretching their wings and that they would soon settle down. Unlike the other staff, he appeared to be unfazed by this.

After breakfast the following morning, they were once again reminded that they were in a foreign country, were representing the college, that rules were different, and the police were much more stringent than in the UK. He hoped that these stern warnings would register sooner rather than later. He proceeded to take his select group out into the city to show them how to use the transport system, purchase single tickets or a carnet. (a book of tickets) He instructed them on how to use them on all modes of transport, including the rapid transport system. They were also given a full orientation of the city. He then returned to the hotel to catch up on lost sleep.

Later that day, around 3.30pm, his sleep was interrupted by a phone call. At the end of the phone came a heavy Scottish accent.

"My name is Harvey McMillan from the British Embassy; do you have a Fraser MacDonald on a trip with you?"

The name was unfamiliar, he needed to check the art students list. He quickly found the name and acknowledged this to the official. Never one to apportion blame, Dave's immediate response was,

"What's he done?"

"Well, he hasn't done anything."

Having piqued his curiosity further, Dave enquired,

"What do you want me to do?"

"Well, do you know the 17th Arrondissement?"

He didn't but quickly stated that if he was told the name and precise location, then he could find it without too much trouble. With that, he was given the address of the Police station in the vicinity. The offer of help was repeated. This was politely declined.

"No, it's fine, I'll be alright."

"Aye, we'll see."

Dave made the trip across the city and arrived at the police station. As the student was under eighteen, Dave, as the responsible adult attached to him, had to withstand the wrath of the Parisian Police, not the student in the station or his fellow students who had abandoned him. Poor Dave was still suffering from a lack of sleep and didn't take this dressing down well at all.

Outside the police station, Dave began to question Fraser,

"What happened then?"

"Well, I got lost."

"Why didn't you just stay with the other students?"

"We were in one of the buildings and I was looking at the architecture and I got lost. I couldn't find anybody."

"But you were picked up at the other end of Paris in the underground, in the Metro."

"Yeah."

"How did you get there?"

"Well, I got on a train."

"Why did you get on a train if you were lost?"

"Well, I thought I might recognise a station if I saw it."

He hadn't grasped how big the city of Paris was and just how many stations there were, unlike Sheffield with its one main station. Having spent an insurmountable amount of time on the train, the poor guy must have been petrified and felt that he had no alternative but to ask for help at the police station.

GET ROB

The tour mantra:

Can I solve this myself?

Can my buddy help me solve it?

Can the captain help?

Where there is no obvious solution: "Get Rob."

This mantra has been perfected over several trips, both home and abroad.

Like much of the British public, Rob, most of the Sports Department and the students, were keen football enthusiasts both on and off the pitch. Football was in their blood. If the staff were not careful, it could totally consume the whole of their lessons without having delved into the curriculum, or if staff were clever, they would find as many ways as possible to speak with authority about their favourite teams whilst teaching, thus earning a generous amount of kudos.

September was the month dedicated to the sports trials. Unlike many of the sports where there was barely sufficient interest to make up a team, the football team trials were fiercely contested and often resulted in the creation of at least four teams. To maintain these it required extra staffing, regular training and all the accoutrements that accompanied match fixtures. This was the norm for the college and Rob wanted to challenge himself to something a little different. He decided to combine his love of the 'glorious game,' with his other love, travel, thus creating his niche. In terms of travel, Europe was too obvious and too close, so America became his destination of choice; it was as yet an uncharted territory for him, so discovering new adventures could only add to the challenge.

The tours were so successful that they became a staple in the college diary. Over the years, the teams visited Tennessee, North Carolina and Virginia regularly and formed lasting relationships with both the players and their coaches.

Many of the boys had never been out of Sheffield before; a night out in Chesterfield, a small town ten miles away, would have been a highlight for them. Or for the lucky minority, the Spanish resorts of Malaga or Magaluf, as was the trend at the time. This was then to be their trip of a lifetime. To see their faces light up at the sights and sounds of those strange places made all of the anxieties of organising the trips worthwhile. For many of the staff and coaches, these trips were the highlight of their careers too.

This particular trip involved thirty young boys travelling across a few states in the USA. All of these boys were young steelworkers and apprentices studying Engineering and Business.

Once they had progressed through the airport and found their seats on their private bus, Rob used to walk down the aisle looking at their faces to capture how enthralled they were at the site of the drive through Manhattan and over the Brooklyn Bridge.

They were enraptured as they gazed out of the windows, drinking in the New York scenery, having never previously travelled out of their home cities.

They were staying at the YMCA at 356 West 34th Street and would have to endure the fourteen-hour-long bus ride journey from New York to Tennessee on the next phase of their journey. An overnight stop could have been made but this would have made a substantial dent in their budget. Rob had managed to strike a great deal with all of the university teams. Not only had he managed to provide buddies for the students, but he also successfully negotiated free accommodation within each university. This included the Universities of Tennessee, North Carolina and Wilson College.

The centre of Manhattan was their first port of call.

It can be quite daunting, and overwhelming for a visitor with the subways: the noise, the lights, the height of the buildings, the hustle and bustle and the glitz and glam. Everyone appears to be in a rush, and no one will speak to you. There could be no greater contrast particularly when you've come from a slow-paced, ambling city where strangers stopped and chatted, passing the time of day with you making you feel welcome. Where the ample green spaces of home entice you to relax, take a moment and breathe. New York appeared to be a complete antithesis to this. It assaulted your senses at high-speed leaving your anonymity intact.

The party arrived on a Saturday in the early evening.

Everyone had been allocated single rooms in the YMCA.

These big strapping 18–21-year-old apprentices and steelworkers, who were super confident and ruled the roost back at home, were shit scared in the unfamiliar territory.

Armed with his checklist of students' names and their room numbers, as per protocol, Rob began to check that the occupants were residing in each of their allocated rooms. He needed reassurances that:

1. they were present.
2. any prior room damage was noted and reported to reception.

What he came across when he entered one of the rooms was alien to his thoughts and was such an unfamiliar sight that he stalled at the entrance. There in front of him bunked up together on a single bed were three of the boys. They were frightened of being on their own. Once Rob had deciphered the issues and set their minds at ease, they eventually returned to their assigned rooms.

They arrived early in the evening on a Saturday after a long journey. The time difference between GMT and EST, the boy's excitement and anxieties, coupled with fatigue could only assist in their decreased presence of mind. Despite being advised of the impending pre-orientation meeting, two of the boys couldn't contain their excitement and set out on a little impromptu adventure. They hadn't ventured far, in fact, they were on the same block as their accommodation when they came across a news-stand. Saturday was the allocated day for the local sports paper to be bought in Sheffield and they didn't want to miss out on their weekly fix. They approached the vendor and asked:

"'as The Green Un come in yet?"

For those of you who are now perplexed as to the meaning of the question, they were enquiring about the Sheffield-produced sports paper... it was green.

The vendor, obviously unaccustomed to this type of approach and accent with tones that could have been mistaken for being slightly aggressive, responded:

"What? What do ya mean? What fucking Green Un?"

The boys were perplexed and insistent.

"The Green Un, yer know The Green Un!"

Exasperated he replied, "No, I don't have a fucking Green Un."

"'ave you got any English papers then?"

"They're all fucking English, what do you mean?"

This banter ping-ponged from one party to the next, with neither having any luck with the other's vernacular.

Eventually, one of the boys turned to his mate and stated,

"Mind you, it dun't get to Rothrum [the town of Rotherham] until ten past six, so it'll probably tek a bit longer to get o'r 'ere."

They returned to their rooms very disgruntled.

To coin an old phrase: 'You can take the boys out of Sheffield, but you can't take Sheffield out of the boys.'

***

A room had been pre-booked for a quick orientation meeting with the boys before they explored the city. Rob explained how the city was set out in terms of its grid and block system. He didn't want them to wander too far, so they were instructed to remain in one block. He had arranged for them to watch a basketball match in the Madison Square Gardens area later that evening. He hoped that the game would entice them enough to return as instructed. He'd thought this through; he needed them to stay in the local vicinity to enable the staff to react to any issues quickly should they occur.

The game was to be viewed in the basement of a little two-storey Italian restaurant/pizza bar. The rules were a little different on this side of the pond; the minimum drinking age was twenty-one, whereas in the UK it was eighteen, so it was going to be interesting managing this from the outset. A quiet word was had with the manager regarding alcohol consumption; he agreed that if the staff were there, were supervising and situations were managed, then the boys were free to drink in the controlled space.

With the meeting over, they were released onto the tiny block around their accommodation. The boys were keen to explore the city and relished a little freedom away from their coaches' eagle eyes. The coaches also felt the need for a little downtime; a much-needed drink or two would help them to relax into the trip. This idea had to be swiftly pushed aside when two of the squad came rushing down the stairs. One of them entered the bar with an excited expression on his face and exclaimed,

"You'll never believe what just 'appened?"

He didn't bother to wait for a reply.

"I've been outside like, and this bloke came up to me and said to me,

Hey man, you wanna buy some good shit?"

 Well, I wer' teken aback and I said,

"What's tha mean do I wanna buy some good shit?"

He said again,

"Do you wanna buy some good shit? I can sell you some good shit."

"I thought me luck were in, so I asked 'im how much it wer'."

"$5 for it, brother."

"I wer' gobsmacked. Do you know what I told 'im?" "Oh, you can get fucking big bags for £1.00 in Rothrum."

He looked at his audience and broke into a broad smile, seemingly pleased with his retort.

***

In between the YMCA and a pizzeria, was a store. To put it bluntly, an adult store.

Within the shop, there were dolls, videotapes, sex toys and pictures of women in various stages of undress with a number of appliances.

In the bowels of the store were small booths, not too dissimilar to photo booths. Having paid the required amount of money, the customer would then be presented with a more personal performance.

The boys were smartly turned out, when they were in the Italian bar, their blazers, embossed with their soccer logos, were attracting attention, not always from the kind that their coaches were happy with. They were learning to adjust swiftly and soaked up their moment in the limelight.

Due to their levels of travelling inexperience, Rob realised that the boys would constantly ask similar questions. As the number of students on the team steadily grew, he realised that he could not be available for every eventuality. To prevent this constant bombardment, he created a set of golden rules or codes that were shared with them.

They were always paired up, so one of their peers became their buddy.

The rules have had minor changes over time. These became their tour mantras.

Rule 1: When out and about, never be without your buddy. Rules 2-5 were more in the form of tasks that followed sequentially from the first. If there's something you don't know, or you want to know, you need to ask yourself a set of questions.

Rule 2: The first question is, can I solve this myself? If the answer to that question is no, then refer to the next question.

Rule 3: Can my buddy help me solve it? If that remained unsolved...then,

Rule 4: Ask the team captain. Only when you've gone through that process and where there is no other solution. Then...

Rule 5: "Get Rob."

These were straightforward and simple enough to follow even in times of distress.

Everyone had regrouped in the Italian Bar and was having a good time, chatting, and drinking beer. The screens were showing American football and basketball.

The party was happy to mingle with the locals and soak up the atmosphere. The locals were engaged in conversations and as usual, commented on how much they loved the British accent, encouraging them to engage in conversation further just to hear how the words were pronounced.

Over the course of the evening, Rob noticed that the group had thinned out somewhat. During the next hour, slowly but surely, he noted that the bar had been emptied of all of the football team. This scenario didn't feel quite right. Rob, the three coaches and a few American customers were all that remained. He didn't have long to consider his possible actions.

Out of the blue, the team captain, Tony, came bursting into the bar.

"Rob, Rob, come quick. Come quick. You need to come quick."

"Why what's happened?"

"It's Mark. Come quick. Come quick. He's got stuck; he's got stuck."

"What do you mean he's got stuck?"

Not waiting for a reply, Rob quickly followed Tony with the three coaches in tow.

He headed towards the YMCA and into the shop next door.

The adult-only shop.

As they entered through its doors, they were momentarily phased by its content. Having adjusted, they made their way through the shop. The assortment of goods on offer swiftly increased the further they delved through its main section. At the entrance, the items appeared to be quite mild and inoffensive, much within the realms of the public's imagination. There were dolls displayed in various stages of undress, then towards the rear of the shop, there were a variety of toys and video screens.

At the far end of the shop there appeared to be separate doors in a circular fashion, implying that there were other forms of entertainment on offer once the customer had entered within.

To enter the inner sanctum, the customer had to pay a dollar. This was exchanged for a token, which was then slotted in the door. This allowed the door to be opened. Once inside, the customer locked the door, securing himself from any external intruders, thus allowing a modicum of privacy. As soon as the door was locked, a transparent screen would lift. The screen was approximately the size of the average adult's head. The customer could then sit alone in their comfortable chair and watch the show.

Inside the arena sat a topless woman.

She was knitting.

Business had been slow.

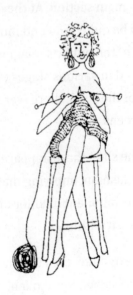

Once the screen had arisen, she would set to work by standing in front of the customer and jiggle her breasts for about two or three minutes. As soon as the customer's money ran out, the screen would shut, thus signalling the end of the show. The customer would then unlock the door and exit the booth.

What appeared to have happened is that two of the boys had discovered the peep show whilst browsing through the shop. They had then hastily returned to the bar to report their findings to the rest of the team.

"You won't believe it but there's a woman and she's got no clothes on."

You can just imagine how much they were trying to contain their excitement. They couldn't afford to raise staff suspicions, so they planned their exits with care and completed this one by one. The last student must have drawn the short straw and had to endure being the thirtieth in the queue. Huge efforts must have been made on his behalf to act nonchalantly whilst chomping at the bit, it must have been torturous. Slowly but surely the bar had emptied.

It was a slow business day, imagine this woman's surprise and delight when out of nowhere, every single screen suddenly opened.

There in front of her were these spotty young faces fully turned out in matching uniformed blazers with the UK's Union Flag embossed on their breast pockets. They were all eagerly peering through at her. She soon realised that a great money-making opportunity had suddenly presented itself. She quickly switched into performance mode and as each screen opened, she began to jiggle her breasts in front of each boy. She quickly moved on to each one zipping around as fast as she could to maintain their attention and enthusiasm. As the money quickly ran out, the screens slammed shut, each boy unlocked their door and speedily returned, having paid for another show.

There were about sixteen screens all fully occupied by the soccer team. She was very busy. One of the boys began to feel a little brave.

"Can I touch your tits?"

She happily agreed,

"For $1."

The money was quickly found and passed through the hatch. He put his hand in and ecstatically touched and squeezed as much as he could for his dollar. Upon noting the additional service, the other boys quickly followed suit, waving their dollar bills and enthusiastically shouting,

"Over 'ere luv, over 'ere, I'll give you a dollar."

The money would again run out and they would repeat the ritual and return to extend their time.

Eventually, one bold young man decided that he would take this a step further. He kindly asked,

"Can I lick your breasts?"

"$5."

He quickly found the cash, handed it over and, eagerly stuck his head under the screen that had now miraculously provided him sufficient access and started to lick away.

He was happily lost in his own world.

His money then ran out.

The screen and shutter came sliding down on his neck, trapping his head in the arena, whilst leaving his body in the booth. The door was locked from the inside. With his legs wiggling and jiggling he tried to decrease the pressure on his neck in an effort to ease his discomfort. He realised that all was lost and had to admit defeat.

The codes fleetingly played through his head. He had no alternative than to omit the first four and shouted for all he was worth,

"Get Rob!"

Rob duly arrived with his support team.

Having seen his predicament, the woman quickly moved on to the remaining boys in their booths with her breasts still jiggling. Eventually one of the lads on the other side said to her,

"Look, love, 'ere's $10, go an' sit down for twenty minutes. It's much funnier watching 'im wi' 'is head stuck in there."

It took some time to get him released.

Rob's arrival swiftly brought with it another dilemma; when he first arrived, he still had no idea of what the issue was. The information that they had received was garbled, verging on hysteria, so he knew that it had to be a serious matter. They arrived at the inner sanctum; in front of them they noted a circle of booths, Tony, the team captain banged on a door with his fist, signalling his return. There came a fumbling noise from the other side of the door, swiftly followed by a sliding sound, then the door swiftly swung ajar. Peter tumbled out and avoiding eye contact, he signalled for Rob to enter. Putting all thoughts aside on the moral nature of the establishment, Rob ducked his head and entered the booth. His senses were overloaded with the views in front of him. Initially, his eyes were drawn to the topless woman in the middle of the room, who appeared to be picking up knitting needles and balls of wool. This did not make any sense. Out of the corner of his eye, his head turned to what appeared to be a disembodied head with a transparent screen around its neck. The jiggling and tongue movements signalled to Rob that he was ok, but in some level of discomfort, or was it embarrassment? A quick scan of the room revealed that Mark, and not the sex worker, was now the star of the show. All eyes were on him. The sex worker had lost her audience. Rob quickly exited the booth, his face communicating to the coaches that this was not one to be missed. One by one, each coach entered the booth, they each left a different person.

This experience has been retold multiple times over the years.

The team were not going to let Mark off lightly, he would be the butt of many jokes for the duration of the trip, but he needed to be released. It quickly emerged that the shop staff would need to be engaged in the rescue. This melodrama propelled Rob into a flurry of activity and he quickly swung into action.

The member of staff summoned to the booths was not too happy, his face elicited a look of minor irritation; perhaps this wasn't the first incident of this kind. After a momentary pause to study the unfortunate student, he considered the possibilities. He settled on dismantling the lock and adjusting the hydraulics systems.

Having received the bill for the damages, Rob wondered how on earth he was going to complete the insurance form, never mind how he was going to explain this to the college managers. These thoughts were placed at the back of his mind, to be reviewed on his return.

With the previous episode still fresh in his memory, Rob now knew that he had his work cut out for the duration of the trip. The opportunities to participate in antics seemed endless. The staff would need to keep a closer eye on all of them. A thought rapidly entered his mind, maybe they'd learned their lesson and that might be the end to their escapades... that quickly vaporised. They were a great group of lads, who just happened to be experimenting and expressing themselves on their first trip abroad, and what a place to do it.

He would save the reprimanding for another time. Experience had taught him that it might initially result in a little peace, but it wouldn't last the course. He was convinced that there was more to come.

The following day, the Greyhound bus arrived to take the team down to Tennessee.

Tennessee's very strict alcohol rules dictated that there was to be no open drinking in public. This rule was explained in no uncertain terms to the team whilst travelling to their destination.

One night in Knoxville, Tennessee, three of the team had been taken out to a few bars by some of the University students. They were sold pitchers of Jack Daniels and coke and inevitably became inebriated.

Before leaving the last bar, they bought six gallons of Budweiser with the idea of consuming them at their residence. Having walked a little way down the road, they found that their drunken conversations needed a little additional lubrication. They proceeded to sit on a wall to drink the alcohol.

Whilst sitting on the wall, the boys were approached by the local constabulary and were duly questioned.

Interpreting the answers was a little difficult for two reasons:

- They were drunk.
- Their strong regional accents.

They were getting nowhere with their line of questioning. Eventually, the police officers mentioned underage drinking and asked if they knew the rules. With the unfortunate combination of alcohol and what can sometimes be misinterpreted as a gruff accent, one of the boys answered a little too quickly, resulting in being hit over the head with a truncheon.

They were all put in the van, arrested and placed in the drunk tank downtown. At 3am the following morning, Rob received a phone call. The caller asked his name and whether he was the soccer coach of the college boys that they had in their custody. Having answered positively, the caller responded,

"Well, we've got three of your boys arrested for drinking alcohol. So, are you gonna come down and get them?"

Rob's response was not as expected.

"Yeah, I'll come down in the morning between ten and eleven o'clock. Leave them there overnight, it will be a good learning experience for them."

Unsurprisingly, the police were happy to comply.

At precisely 11 am, the coaches arrived at the police station, their anticipation mingled with concern. As they approached the holding area, they were taken aback to see one of their players sporting a rather large and ominous bruise on his head. The sight heightened their worries. The police officers hurriedly gathered the players and marched them out of their cells. The players stood before the coaches, their blazers clutched tightly under their arms, wearing expressions that revealed both anxiety and relief.

Silence filled the air.

The boys hung their heads. One by one they explained their demeanours. The winos in the drunk tank had taken a liking to the blazers and been attempting to acquire them as souvenirs. The barrage continued throughout the night. To defend themselves, the boys had to remain awake fending off attacks from the American detainees.

A night in the cells was enough to quell any further ideas of any adventurous behaviour. From that moment on, no further reprimand was needed.

The tours were such a hit, that the boys at home and abroad, still have reunions to this day.

***

Every lecturer in the sports department knew Paul's name. It was not because he was studious; it was more of a case of him being a 'misunderstood young man.' They just didn't get him. He was caught in the familiar merry-go-round of trying everything until he found something that suited him. He had no clear career goals… Well, he had no goals at all. At present he was a motor vehicle student and, as an additional subject, he also opted to pursue General Studies. Unfortunately, this took place in the last teaching session on Friday afternoons, the aptly named 'Graveyard slot.' This arrangement became forged within the motor vehicle department's history. The boys used to return from their lunch break via an extended time in the pub, imbibing as much alcohol as they could within the narrow period. As can be extracted, vehicle maintenance and alcohol were not the best bedfellows.

In those days, Paul was often described as being a little 'off the wall.' A career as a car mechanic was not to be in his future. He was quite hopeless as evidenced by the failure of all of his mechanics exams. But he had character.

Rob, now a senior lecturer, happened to be in the staffroom one Friday afternoon. The General Studies lecturer burst through the staffroom door and exclaimed:

"That's it, I'm finished, I'm done. I'm not doing it anymore. I'm not teaching that bunch of rabble. They're absolute lunatics. I'm not having anything to do with them. I've left them in the classroom down there."

The only response that Rob could give was to encourage him to open up and discuss the issues with him.

"Why? What's the matter?"

"They're just mad, absolutely mad."

Rob thought that as the most senior member of staff present, he ought to investigate the claim. This specific classroom happened to be towards the end of a long corridor. As he suspected, he could hear them before he could see them. The din was unusual as it carried an equine resonance to it. Upon reaching the room, he dared only to peep through the window, lest he was detected. Their behaviour had left nothing to the imagination, and it didn't take a genius to identify that they were very intoxicated. This deliberate breach of the rules was not the only problem, there was also a small matter of their attire. It was unsuitable for their course of study. Rob couldn't decide whether they had visited a fancy-dress shop before or after the pub. Either way, there, on full display were four horse's heads on the bodies of the students.

Paul appeared to be the ringleader.

There they were, sitting in their rows in the classroom, having refused to take off their headgear. The poor teacher had tried every method in the training handbook to continue his lesson. Each time he opened his mouth to address the class, out would come,

"Neigh, neigh."

One student's behaviour was rapidly followed by the other three. The poor man never stood a chance. Who knows what had gone through his head when the horse-clad students proceeded to enter the room and take their seats? He should have been applauded for even attempting to begin a lesson as it was obvious from the outset that this was a non-starter. Eventually, he came to his senses and gave up.

Rob quietly observed the riot unfolding in the classroom whilst internally acknowledging the teacher's obvious state of distress. He left the scene unnoticed and walked towards the cafe with an idea forming in his head. He approached the cafe manager and asked if he had an unwanted cardboard box that he could use. Once he had been given this, he cut out two eye holes, a nose and a place for his mouth. He then placed the box on his head. He retraced his steps down the corridor and walked unannounced into the class. He identified Paul and lined himself up in front of him. Slowly he bent his head down towards him. Their eyes contacted through their disguises.

"I'm your new General Studies teacher."

Paul had found his new leader. He deferred his antics and instantly fell into line. Having noted the shift in Paul's demeanour, the others swiftly followed suit. Friday afternoon General Studies lessons quickly became de rigueur, minus the alcohol and fancy dress.

A year or so later, one of the English teachers happened to have a serendipitous conversation with her husband. She needed some inspiration for her English class and her husband was a good friend of Ken Loach, the English film director. At the time, he was in the process of creating a new film entitled 'Raining Stones.' He was also looking for a few Sheffield boys to play local character roles. She couldn't let this opportunity pass her by. Using her husband as the intermediary, she invited him into college to talk to her students. The kudos earned for the college would always come in handy. Ken was happy to oblige, his agenda wasn't exactly hidden and what could be better than the genuine article for his new film?

On the pre-arranged date, he arrived, gave a talk on the film industry and the usage of language within it. He ended by asking if there were any local 'lively and laddish' boys who would be available for auditions in his new film. Rob heard about this during the unusually elevated chats in the staffroom and immediately thought of Paul as a good fit for the role. Paul, always up for a challenge and having nothing to lose, decided to attend the audition. Little did he know that this would be the turning point in his life as he finally found his true vocation and was offered a part in the film.

He went on to act in some of the most notable regional soap operas in England. When the opportunities arose, he progressed onto British films, often playing the part of police officers: 'the not quite innocent types.' He was a natural, he didn't act, he just played himself, it was a little of 'life imitating art.' To add to his back catalogue, he went on to write a major film and reached the giddy heights of acting fame by appearing in a respectable role in Rogue One: A Star Wars Story in 2016.

It had been at least twenty years since Rob had any communication with Paul, but he had keenly tracked his acting progression with pride. Having observed him in his biggest role to date, he messaged Paul to express his congratulations. By way of an introduction, his message began with his impressions of the film, how wonderful it was and how much he enjoyed his acting too. To jog his memory, he went on to state,

"I don't know if you remember me, but I was your General Studies teacher."

Paul responded with a personalised message.

"I remember you really well, warmly and with affection because you were the only one who really got me."

What an accolade to have from a former student who could so easily have fallen by the wayside.

Rob went on to recall the numerous former students who have contacted him over the decades, usually recalling their sporting days and tours with him, thanking him for the opportunities and the experiences that they now recall with fondness, and how he gave them the confidence to aim high and fulfil their dreams.

These are the moments that have kept Rob upbeat in his retired years, knowing that those boys who might have been brushed off and labelled as 'no-hopers,' are now proud, mature, and responsible middle-aged men who continue to freely express their gratitude to him for rescuing them all those years ago.

And really, isn't that what being a teacher is all about?

ACKNOWLEDGEMENTS

To David Fenton, for continuing to provide me with your technical help. You're my rock.

Aileen Jarrett-Ward, Margaret Chapman, Janine Roberts and Holly Bradley, thank you for your critical eye and for politely keeping me on the straight and narrow.

To all of the wonderful people with whom I've been re acquainted with and those who have shared common and new stories with me, I thank you. You have reminded me of my early teaching days and the camaraderie of years gone by. A special mention goes to Dave Eyre, Bob Harrison and John Birks for sharing your stories.

To my former pupils, the class of 2MB, what a wonderful bunch of women you are. I am privileged to meet you in your adult lives and am honoured to be in your presence.

REVIEWS

"Well done on writing another hilarious and heart-warming book!"
R Wojturska

If you want truthful, humorous, insightful or close to the knuckle accounts of the everyday tales from our nation's educators, this is the book for you. I laughed, cried and on so many occasions punched the air with a hearty "Yes!" Students are students whatever their shoes size. The contents of this book will resonate with all those who dare to teach.
A Ward

More entertaining anecdotes and observations from Maxine. Guaranteed to trigger memories from your own school days!

Ten minutes to spare? Grab a cuppa and enjoy!
M. Chapman

If you want to hear more about my next adventures, you can sign up the following ways:

1. My website at maxineblake.com

Or follow me at

2. https://www.facebook.com/maxine.blake.921/
3. https://www.instagram.com/maxine.blake.921/

Finally

Reviews are one of the most powerful tools that help authors to gain the attention of new readers.

If you enjoyed my book, I would be very grateful if you could spend a few minutes leaving a review (it doesn't have to be long and may only take 2 minutes)

Thank you so much.

ABOUT THE AUTHOR

Maxine Blake is of Jamaican descent and was born and raised in Wolverhampton in the UK. She has dedicated 37 years of her life to teaching and held management positions within educational settings before retiring in 2020. She holds a Master of Education degree.

In her retirement, Maxine remains active both nationally and internationally within education. She also maintains her passion for singing with the Sheffield Community Choir and continues to diligently hone her piano skills.

Maxine has rekindled her love for international travel as a solo female adventurer and has authored several guided journals to assist other women who aspire to embark on similar journeys.

"Teacher Bloopers and Potty Mouth Stories" serves as the sequel to her previous work, "Don't Poo in the Pudding Bowl."

She currently resides in Sheffield with her husband.

Printed in Great Britain
by Amazon